CW01654055

CRA

Beáta Kalamár

# CRAFT LEADERSHIP

Sharpen the REAL LEADER in YOU
by mobilising
the 5 CRAFT Leadership qualities

CRAFT Leadership: Sharpen the REAL LEADER in YOU
by mobilising the 5 CRAFT Leadership qualities by Beáta Kalamár

First published in 2022
by PALLAS ATHÉNÉ KÖNYVKIADÓ KFT.,
Úri utca 21, 1014 Budapest, Hungary
dr. Katinka Cseh, CEO

www.pallasathenekiado.hu



Edited by Paula Lévay



Typeset by Anita Kónya
Printed in 2022
by Copy & Consulting Kft.
Budapest, Hungary
Zsolt Gál, CEO

ISBN 978-963-573-125-1

# TABLE OF CONTENTS


**PREFACE** **ix**

How CRAFT Leadership was born ix
How to get the most out of this book xiii
Feedback xiii

**ACKNOWLEDGEMENTS** **xv**

**INTRODUCTION** **1**

My definition of leadership 1
Leader vs manager 2
Leadership quality 3
What makes a high-quality leader? 4
What is this book about? 7
What trends will impact the future of leadership? 9

**CHAPTER I**
**Sharpen the REAL LEADER in you** **11**

The REAL LEADER: What does REAL mean in the context of leadership? 11
The importance of self-awareness 13
A leader's projected image 18
The authentic self as a leader 24
The value-driven leader 27
Integrity 31
A high-level introduction to the CRAFT model 39

**CHAPTER II**

**C is for CREATIVITY and CREATE** 41

The business context of CREATIVITY for today and tomorrow 41
The theory of CREATIVITY 45
The CREATIVITY cocktail – How to develop CREATIVITY 51
CREATIVITY and continuous improvement 65
CREATIVITY and innovation 65
CREATIVITY and strategy 68
The leader as a CREATOR 76
CRAFTING the future 77

**CHAPTER III**

**R is for RESILIENCE** 81

The definition and importance of RESILIENCE 81
The resilient leader 87
The resilient organisation 92
Threats to RESILIENCE and strategies to cope 93
Flexibility in thinking to enhance RESILIENCE 98
Flexibility in feeling to embrace your inner RESILIENCE 100
Being resourceful is the road to RESILIENCE 103
Anchors as the rocks underneath RESILIENCE 104
Skilful energy management in mastering RESILIENCE 106

**CHAPTER IV**

**A is for AGILITY** 117

The meaning of AGILITY 117
Why AGILITY matters so much today 118
The agile leader 122
AGILITY starts with thinking 129
Working with AGILITY – The power of Neuro-Agility 130
Whole-brain leadership for AGILITY 142

**CHAPTER V**

**F is for FOCUS** 147

Why FOCUS matters so much in leadership today 147
Today's challenges for leaders in FOCUS 149
The functionality dimension of leadership FOCUS 153

Pareto Principle (20/80) and leadership FOCUS 159
A systemic approach to leadership FOCUS 164
Flexibility in FOCUS 169
Managing self-limiting tendencies in leadership FOCUS 175

**CHAPTER VI**

**T is for TRUST** **185**

What is happening with TRUST today? 185
The importance of TRUST 187
What makes a trustworthy leader according to the leaders I interviewed? 190
TRUST in self/TRUST self 192
TRUST others – one to one and one-to-many: teams 195
The Trust equation 197
TRUST in economic terms 214
TRUST in emotional terms 214
TRUST others – one to many: organisations and networks 215
TRUST in the unknown 219
TRUST in gratitude 221

**CHAPTER VII**

**Inside Journey - the leader in you**
**What makes you a unique and powerful leader?** **223**

Pulling it all together - What is your CRAFT? 223
CREATIVITY and CREATE Mind Map 226
CREATIVITY and CREATE – Summary of Reflection Questions 227
CREATIVITY and CREATE – Self-Assessment 228
RESILIENCE Mind Map 230
RESILIENCE – Summary of Reflection Questions 231
RESILIENCE – Self-Assessment 232
AGILITY Mind Map 234
AGILITY – Summary of Reflection Questions 235
AGILITY – Self-Assessment 236
FOCUS Mind Map 238
FOCUS – Summary of Reflection Questions 239
FOCUS – Self-Assessment 241

TRUST Mind Map 244
TRUST – Summary of Reflection Questions 245
TRUST – Self-Assessment 247
The pinnacle of your CRAFT journey 249

**CHAPTER VIII**
**Outside Journey - Leading your organisation**
**How do you steer your CRAFT? 251**
Putting into practice 251
The metaphor 252
Exploring your leadership with a metaphor 253
The impact of your CRAFT Leadership 256

**CHAPTER IX**
**Keep sharpening the REAL LEADER in you**
**to be fit for the future 257**
Reinforcing CRAFT Leadership 257

**REFERENCES 265**

**LIST OF ILLUSTRATIONS 273**

**ABOUT THE AUTHOR 275**

# PREFACE

## How CRAFT Leadership was born

I have been working in adult education, specifically in corporate learning and development, for the last 20 years of my career. Leadership has become my main focus area; I am particularly fascinated by and passionate about it.

About 8 years ago, I attended a webinar presented by Myles Downey, founder of The School of Coaching in the UK. It was particularly special for me because Myles is one of the many reasons I became a coach in 2002. But that's a different story.

When I participated in this particular webinar, Myles asked two questions to prepare us for the twenty-first century: *What is your craft? What makes you a unique and powerful coach?* These questions stuck in my mind. They kept rolling around, coming back again, and again, day after day. It wasn't just because my searching for answers to these questions was so important for me at that time of my life; somehow, they occupied my mind so hauntingly that I don't know how and when they became part of my coaching discussions with leaders. I started asking them the very same questions: What is your craft as a leader? What makes you a unique and powerful leader? That was the early sign of the birth of CRAFT Leadership.

I've heard from many leadership gurus and experts that leadership is not a title. It's not a position. It's an action, a series of actions, a process, or a journey. Leadership 10 years ago was not what it is today and will not be the same 10 years from now. I agree with them.

As I see it, leadership is an ever-changing and evolving craft (CRAFT). A leadership journey from apprenticeship to mastery is a journey with milestones that has no end to it and has no shortcuts. Getting there will take time and require extra miles. From my 20 years of experience as an executive coach, I have learnt that there are many different paths. Not one of them is the same. How come? Because we live in an ever-changing reality with increased uncertainty and disruption. These conditions require leaders to continuously develop themselves and sharpen their leadership qualities. But why do I call them leadership qualities and what qualities are we talking about here? We'll explore this a little bit later.

Today's world is so volatile that the saying from Heraclitus is more relevant than ever: No man ever steps into the same river twice [...]. Therefore, taking your current leadership position for granted is a huge mistake. It is never static, as people's interactions are dynamic, constantly changing and evolving.

Tenure (time and work experience) does not matter in the way it mattered in the past. It no longer guarantees that those leaders who don't make the effort to develop themselves purposefully will be in position for long. On this journey of self-development, you need to find your way of doing it, and design your journey to becoming a crafted/CRAFTed leader.

Why? Because, according to John C. Maxwell (2013:44), "The only way to improve an organisation is to grow and improve the leaders."

While working with many leaders, I noticed recurring patterns and trends in our conversations:

- I must become a more visionary leader; that is what my board expects from me.
- I should generate more innovation within the organisation, and I should determine my role in this.
- I am struggling with multitasking; there are so many things on my plate. Prioritising is becoming harder and harder.
- I have an enormous workload with many challenges. My life is really stressful; I am almost at the edge of burnout.
- I've started losing the sparkle in my eyes and losing my own why.
- I need to build relationships not only in my own organisation but across the region, globally, and in the market. This is time-consuming and I am very much out of my comfort zone.
- I feel the trust around me is so fragile. I sometimes try to get people on my side by using more authority but without success.
- I have to build a function, an organisation that can rapidly respond to the needs of the market.

These pain points fall in place and are structured around the 5 leadership qualities this book presents to you. I created CRAFT in 2015 and since then, it has evolved along with the changing business environment.

We are living in very interesting times; economic, environmental, and geopolitical risks and technological advancements are all coming together. The dynamic of today's business environment is that no one day, or hour, or even minute is the same.

If you don't prepare yourself for the future, you trade off your choice to be a leader who is responsible for their business, their people, their community, and their world. To be able to respond to the needs of these key stakeholders, you need to continually prepare yourself. Our world never stands still; if anything, it is spinning faster and faster.

As there is a limit to how many leaders I can physically work with, the time has come to put pen to paper, to collate my thoughts so that more people can benefit from this solution.

I also want to contribute to the world by emphasising and promoting the importance of having more high-quality leaders with and in decision-making power at the head of companies. With this book, I want to reach out to more leaders and leadership candidates. I want to share my experience of working with leaders for the last 20 years.

What I give you is a snapshot of my solution. But no matter how volatile and disruptive the world is, the fundamentals are pretty much the same. It's like playing with Lego. You can use the same pieces; you only need to reconstruct, to change the outline. You can leave out some pieces or add new ones to make your leadership relevant for today.

What you hold in your hand is a handbook supported by a theory that can become your daily or weekly guide to developing or sharpening the REAL LEADER in you by mobilising the 5 CRAFT Leadership qualities herein.

### *This book is for you if you are...*

- **an experienced senior leader** who needs to sharpen the REAL LEADER in you. Maybe you have lost not only your passion but perhaps even yourself on the road to where you are today.

Maybe your positive impact has been eroded by all the blind spots and skeletons you're hoarding unintentionally.

- **a junior leader or manager who wants to become a leader** and step up your game.
- **starting out** but already know you want to be a future leader.

If your job is to help develop new leaders or help existing leaders develop their potential, you too might find some new perspectives herein.

## How to get the most out of this book

I created this book to be a practical guide and handbook. While reading each chapter, as you read the reflection points answer the questions and highlight those you feel need more time to think about. Perhaps discuss them with someone. At the end of the book, you will have an opportunity to revisit these questions and assess your readiness in CRAFT Leadership.

## Feedback

I welcome your feedback. Email me at *craftleadership@beatakalamar.com*. Perhaps I will share your insights more widely on my leadership blog at *http://beatakalamar.com/blog* so that we can continue to further build practical insights for becoming CRAFTed leaders for today and tomorrow.

# ACKNOWLEDGEMENTS

I am indebted to those who have supported me in writing this book. First, and most importantly, my gratitude goes to Dr habil. Anita Pierog, associate professor, who helped me through this journey with her high academic professionalism and patient kindness. Writing this book was a hard upward climb for me. She was there for me, challenging me, supporting me, motivating me, lifting me up, and occasionally patching me up when I fell to pieces. Her questions, reflections, and feedback kept me going and made this project one of the biggest learning curves in my life.

My enduring thanks also go to my family and friends, especially Gyöngyvér Martin and Judit Ábri, my esteemed colleagues, who were my cheerleaders, my sounding boards, and my thinking partners when I was climbing the walls in desperation and flying high with happiness.

I reached out to a number of leaders, 55 to be exact, who shared their valuable opinions and experiences with me. I am ever so grateful for the time they spent answering my questions and sharing their stories and thoughts. Our conversations were so inspiring and energising that at some point I felt I could carry on having conversations like these forever; they fuelled me and kept me going. My humble hope is that they sharpened their leadership qualities by stopping for 90 minutes and reflecting on their unique style. They not only participated in the co-creation of this book, but I hope will be able to learn from it as well when they read these lines.

Writing about CRAFT Leadership could not have happened without my 20 years of experience supporting leaders with executive coaching and mentoring. The trust my executive and leadership clients have in me, their openness about their challenges, and their feedback helped me become the professional I am right now. Their stories shaped the way I think about leadership and the way I work with leaders today. Thank you all!

I pay tribute and offer thanks to those leaders and leadership experts who moulded my thinking about working with leaders through their books, courses, workshops, and interactions. My role in this world is not to reinvent the wheel, but rather to incorporate their findings and great insights into my work and build on them. They have, albeit unknowingly, also become co-creators of this book.

Finally, I would like to thank Pallas Athéné Books for their professionalism and care in publishing this book. In particular, Katinka Cseh, Managing Director, and Paula Lévay, Chief Editor. They have made my dream of becoming an author come true by publishing my first book. I am so grateful to them.

# INTRODUCTION

"Everything rises and falls on leadership."

Maxwell (2018:16)

## My definition of leadership

There are many definitions of leadership out there. In his book *The Future Leader*, Jacob Morgan (2020) asked 140 CEOs from the world's top organisations to define leadership. They all defined it differently. I don't think the world needs yet another definition, but I do need to clarify what I think and who I mean when I say 'leader' throughout this book.

If I had to choose two of the definitions out there, these two capture my heart the most.

The first is commonly attributed to John Quincy Adams:

> "If your actions inspire others to dream more, learn more, do more and become more, you are a leader."

I'd go so far as to humbly add to this quotation so that it reads:

> "If ***your words*** and actions inspire others to dream more, learn more, do more and become more you are a leader."

The second is from John C. Maxwell (2007:11)

> "Leadership is influence – nothing more, nothing less."

I'd add to this, too, so that it reads:

> "Leadership is ***impact and*** influence – nothing more, nothing less."

The aim is not only to influence others but also to achieve a greater impact on a group of people. Leadership is first and foremost a people business. Without people, there is no leader. Without people, there is no business. People determine the future success of any organisation. There is no artificial intelligence (AI), no robotics, no disruption, no innovation without people.

## Leader vs manager

The other defining factor of leadership for me is where leaders spend most of their time and focus. Unfortunately, more people call themselves leaders than actually are leaders.

Both leaders and managers function in 3 domains: strategy, operation, and development. But the order of importance and the time spent on these domains differ for the two.

A manager's number one priority is in the operation domain: planning, creating budgets, allocating and organising resources, implementing policies and procedures, enforcing controls, solving everyday problems, making everyday decisions, and minimising risks. Their secondary focus is on development: developing their people, the organisation, and the business. The least amount of their time is spent on building a long-term vision and strategizing.

A leader's number one priority is in the strategy domain: looking at the long-term horizon, following global megatrends and industry trends, facilitating discussions about the future, challenging the status quo, creating visions and partnerships, innovating, and connecting the dots. Their second priority is development: developing people – especially leadership teams and key talents – by influencing and inspiring, developing business, developing markets, and developing their organisation. They spend very little of their time on operation: reporting and data analysis. This will be dealt with in more detail in Chapter V: F is for FOCUS.

## Leadership quality

There are reasons behind why I decided to talk about leadership quality and what I really mean by leadership quality. Let's start with some data, which induced my thinking in this direction: "When looking at the financial performance, organisations with the highest quality leaders were 13 times more likely to outperform their industry competitors. These organisations also had higher employee retention and engagement rates up to three times that of their competitors" (Morgan, 2020:32).

According to the Cambridge Dictionary (2021), "the definition of quality is how good or bad something is, a high standard, a degree of excellence, a differentiating factor, what makes someone, or something stand out." I always laugh off the cliché that "Everyone knows a good leader when they see one." And in my experience, people leave companies and organisations because of poor leadership. We all have stories of good leaders and good leadership. We have even more stories about bad leaders and bad leadership. But to decode the good leader or the excellence of leadership is very difficult. Quality is contextual and subjective when it comes to leadership. Can it be measured? How can you capture the essence of a high-quality leader?

Quality could include leadership competence, knowledge, skills, attitude, behaviours, character, mindset, intention, discipline, and habit. Quality is a larger set, which I decided to address.

Why is leadership quality so important? As Maxwell (2018:16) puts it, "Everything rises and falls on leadership."

Another piece of data about leadership quality: "Organisations are facing a significant leadership quality gap. Leaders and human resources are divided on the quality of leadership in their organisations. 48 percent of leaders rate their leadership quality as high, while only 28 percent of human resources share the same belief. As current leaders struggle to meet ongoing changes, HR professionals worry that they don't have the skills to meet future challenges from Global Leadership Forecast" (DDI, 2021). This also shows how hard it is to see what quality really means; it very much depends on who decides what quality is and based on what criteria.

Due to globalisation and technological advancement, the competitive market has opened up. The local labour market is becoming more of a global resource market, where employees are in control and where high-quality leadership is essential in retaining the workforce.

## What makes a high-quality leader?

As part of my research for this book, I carried out 55 interviews with leaders and future leaders in various industries, such as financial, information technology (IT), telecommunications, retail, energy, consulting, manufacturing, pharma, local, regional (especially in the region of Central Eastern Europe), and global roles, and with university students who have leadership potential and ambitions.

Interviewees are from big multinational corporations to small and medium-sized enterprises (SMEs). Their leadership roles vary from global CEOs and directors to regional managing directors to local managing directors and owners, CxOs, and leaders of specific divisions of organisations. As I promised anonymity to the interviewees, I don't use either their names or their company's name. I decided not to use pseudonyms, either. In each chapter, I have compiled various data provided by the interviewees and tailored this data to the topic to represent differences and similarities in opinions. I have also highlighted some specific answers under the leadership insights section.

I asked these leaders to tell me what they think determines a high-quality leader. Some common features emerged.

The high-quality leaders of today and tomorrow must create sustainable companies that are value-driven and provide an authentic vision full of perspectives and stability. Quality leaders are trusted leaders who keep themselves relevant and can achieve influence and impact on a larger scale. To be relevant they must keep learning and be a role model for continuous development. They also need to look for future trends and possibilities. They must have a strong, regularly updated knowledge of the market. As for greater influence and impact, their number one focus should be on people, as they are at the heart of any business. In their service leadership, they should put the company's mission and their people first by empowering them through authenticity and integrity and by enhancing their own credibility with high-quality, versatile communication. Quality leaders are also change-agile, i.e., proactive when it comes to change with a high level of adaptability.

I was once told a story about a leader who didn't have to delegate work or recruit anyone into his team because people wanted to work with him particularly. They volunteered for any work under his leadership. What is high-quality leadership if not this?! One thing is for sure, as one of the leaders I interviewed noted:

> "When it is sunny, it is easy to be a good quality leader. Leadership makes a difference when it's raining, when it's stormy. Today, maybe there are sunny patches but much of it is rather stormy."

Here are some different or not so different yet thought-provoking comments about high-quality leadership given by the interviewees:

> "The quality leader I respected and looked upon was a crafted leader. I felt the craft, the unique power in him."

> "The quality leader doesn't want to take things away; they want to add and to create at all times."

> "It is not a great art to achieve results by exploiting others. Based on research, no common features or qualities can be found among great leaders. There is not much in common between Elon Musk, Napoleon, Steve Jobs, and Mother Teresa (innovator, team player, tyrant, saviour)."

> "We use a metaphor or a symbol: a 3-legged chair is the moststable. If you say too many things, people won't remember them. We can only work with people and leaders who are good; someone who is not a good person cannot be a good quality leader. 1) Especially in our culture, a good person according to our company has a heart. They are honest, loyal, truthful, not manipulative, a philanthropist,

> friendly, and brave. They give immediate feedback, are hungry for success, and want to achieve something. 2) A good quality leader must deliver results in numbers. 3) They must have the ability to develop themselves, be willing to take the risk, understand the importance of continuous learning, want to develop and actually make sure they do. They are good and quality leaders. We always look for 3-legged people and leaders."

> "The mirror effect: how high-quality a leader is, very much depends on how well the organisation performs underneath them and how satisfied the employees are under their supervision. They reflect your level of quality as a leader."

Your response to the question of what makes a good leader may change over time because you mature, you evolve, and the business environment changes, too. And that's okay. Aim to design your way of leadership and create your own map for your leadership journey. Of course, you have to revisit your design from time to time and update or change it but that is what continuous development or life-long learning is about.

## What is this book about?

This book is about CRAFT Leadership, one of the executive solutions I work with. It is about how to advance yourself as a leader by developing the 5 CRAFT Leadership qualities. Throughout this journey, you will improve your team as well because everything in your organisation is based on leadership and team interactions.

Chapter I introduces the motto of CRAFT Leadership. It goes on to explore the importance of being true to your real self as a leader, and the challenges you may face when you distance yourself from your true essence. I also introduce the CRAFT Leadership model at a high level.

In Chapters II to VI, I unfold each CRAFT Leadership quality by laying a foundation through definitions and theories. We'll discuss how these qualities can be developed by better understanding all the elements and through questions and exercises. You'll learn where you should focus to make a shift and achieve mastery in each quality.

Chapter VII pulls everything together by reviewing each quality presented in a mind map. You'll get to revisit the reflection points raised throughout the book and assess yourself against the CRAFT Leadership qualities to help you transfer what you have learnt about yourself as a leader.

In Chapter VIII, you will start putting all these into practice with the help of a metaphor by looking at how you steer your organisation as a craft (ship) on the ocean of today's turbulent world.

Finally, in the last chapter, Chapter IX, I emphasise the importance of sharpening yourself as our world keeps moving on rapidly, at an unrelenting pace.

Each chapter unfolds in various structural parts. The context and theory relate to each quality. Exercises and reflection points show you how you can develop yourself to achieve mastery. I summarise the thinking of the 55 leaders I interviewed and share their thoughts under the heading Leadership insights. I've also included various anecdotes - business, client, or personal stories - related to the topic.

## What trends will impact the future of leadership?

The 55 leaders I interviewed highlighted the main areas they think will influence the future of leadership:

- The VUCA (volatile, uncertain, complex, and ambiguous) world and its ongoing impacts on business and leadership.
- Global megatrends, such as geopolitical shifts, further technological advancements, climate change and scarcity, and changes in demographics.
- Digitalisation and the fast spread of robotics and AI.
- Changes in the labour market, the shortage of skilled labour, generation gaps and challenges in the workplace, destructuring and restructuring of the labour market and ways of working.
- The COVID-19 pandemic and its impacts and long-term after-effects, which may not yet be known.
- Rapid changes in the needs and expectations of different stakeholders.
- Political and geopolitical events that go hand in hand with globalisation and polarisation and their impact on regulations at various levels.
- Ongoing changes and the transformation required to survive and thrive.

These factors create constant disruptions for businesses. As a leader, you need to learn how you can prepare yourself to get ahead of the game and not lag and become a victim of stormy environments.

CRAFT Leadership gives you solid ground to build on. Even in the broad sense, these main areas indicate that there is not much by way of stability around us. You need a quality surfboard to ride those waves. This is what the 5 CRAFT Leadership qualities are designed for.

# CHAPTER I

# Sharpen the REAL LEADER in you

"Stop playing a leader. Be a real leader."

(Scotton, 2018)

## The REAL LEADER: What does REAL mean in the context of leadership?

The motto of CRAFT Leadership: *Sharpen the REAL LEADER in you by mobilising the 5 CRAFT Leadership qualities.*

When I came up with this motto, I thought of two things. First, it is based on my experience of working with leaders and executives. I have seen in almost every case that leaders tend to lose themselves, their REAL SELF, either partly or fully in the job of being a leader, especially when they have been leaders for quite a while. Their position and title can easily become their identity. It is not deliberate or sudden. No one wants this. Sometimes they let their surroundings push them into this trap, for example when their employees can see them and communicate with them only as their CEO without any real human connection or when their key stakeholders/shareholders see them and communicate with them only through their commission to comply with the short-term mandate, i.e., deliver quarterly results. It happens gradually and unnoticed, no matter how smart they are. It becomes their everyday normal.

That is why it is important to build your leadership on solid ground and learn about what can happen when you stop monitoring yourself: you get misaligned and derailed.

In today's business world, with all the disruptions and noise, it is pretty easy to get lost, clouded, and misaligned without any conscious intention. In fierce competition, it is also easy to become 'positional'. Today, everything is about how you position yourself. I once saw a picture in which children were standing in a row and looking over a banister to see the view and what was happening on the other side. The smallest child who, to be able to see at all, stood on the middle section of the banister while the others were standing on the ground. As a result, she became the 'tallest' child with the best view. This picture was speaking about business intelligence. It said that success was not about size, but rather about positioning. While I really liked this image and the message it conveyed at that time, later on, I realised that there is a trap; when you lose connection to your real self, your positioning becomes not only your reality but your identity as well. "When you try to be more than you are, you end up being much less than you could be" (Hanse and Carucci, 2014:35).

I'm not saying that being task- and results-oriented and positioning yourself is wrong; I'm simply saying that it becomes wrong when they become the only determining and controlling factor in your leadership.

Today, there is a greater risk for leaders to disconnect and lose their REAL SELF on the road. Nevertheless, self-aligned, self-connected, authentic leaders have greater influence and power based on and built from the inside out.

The second meaning behind my motto is related to the word 'sharpen'. Leadership is a process, a journey, which requires not only continual effort but also intentionality in developing yourself, constantly checking your REAL SELF and refining and adjusting it in your leadership. Leaders need more learning, more reflection, and more checking than their employees, because the impact of their actions and words is far greater than their people's.

In this chapter, we'll work on sharpening the REAL LEADER in you by covering:

- The importance of self-awareness
- A leader's projected image
- The authentic self as a leader
- The value-driven leader
- Integrity

I'll also give you a high-level introduction to the CRAFT model.

## The importance of self-awareness

To sharpen your knowledge of yourself as a leader is to hone how you should be and how others perceive you; this is what self-awareness means. There is evidence that self-aware leaders can deliver better financial performance; self-awareness can actually lead to more profitable companies (Morgan, 2020).

"When it comes to self-awareness Dr. Tasha Eurich discovered something disturbing: there is an inverse relationship between power and self-awareness. This means that the more senior you become in your organisation, the less self-aware you tend to be. This is exactly why it's so crucial for leaders to practice self-awareness" (Morgan, 2020:207).

The question is where you should look to establish your identity as a leader. At your public image? At your accomplishments? At your recognition? Or do you get it from your internal rocks like your values, your driving force, your passions, your moral compass?

### *Learning about your natural behavioural tendencies*

Greater awareness starts with an accurate perception of yourself as a leader and what impact you have on your environment. It starts with better understanding yourself and others by using a tool. Self-assessments and different types of diagnostic tools help leaders better understand themselves. There are many tools out there. I particularly like using computerised reports for executives about their behaviours.

Imagine you are sitting on the terrace of Café Gerbeaud situated on Vörösmarty tér, a busy square in beautiful Budapest. It's a sunny day. You're alone, having a short mid-day recharge and reflection before your next meeting begins late afternoon. You're feeling pretty content sipping your favourite coffee, enjoying a cake (why not, you deserve it), and watching people. You begin to notice interesting similarities in the people passing by. Although each one looks different physically, there are many similarities in how they act. Some seem talkative and friendly with high and light energy, while others look focused, intense, and business-like. Some talk more than listen, while others just listen. Some appear to be forceful and direct, while others seem patient and relaxed. This is how observable behaviours and behavioural patterns can be found in your own and others' preferences and natural tendencies. This is why I like using DISC (*how* you behave, *how* you act) alongside Motivators/Driving forces (*why* you behave and act, the *way* you behave and act) for profiling leaders and executives. DISC stands for Dominance, Influence or Inspiring, Steadiness or Stability, and Compliance. Each of the 4 behavioural styles has a colour assigned to it (Figure 1.1). DISC is a universal language of observable human behaviours, a natural part of who you are. Some of your behaviours come from nature (inherent) and some others come from nurture (your upbringing). DISC analyses your behavioural styles (natural and adapted). What I also like about it is that it is a neutral language; there is no good or bad. It helps you better understand yourself and learn about your own strengths and weaknesses, about where you are, about how unique you are. It shows you where your potentials lie and where you can unknowingly sabotage your own success (Erikson, 2019).

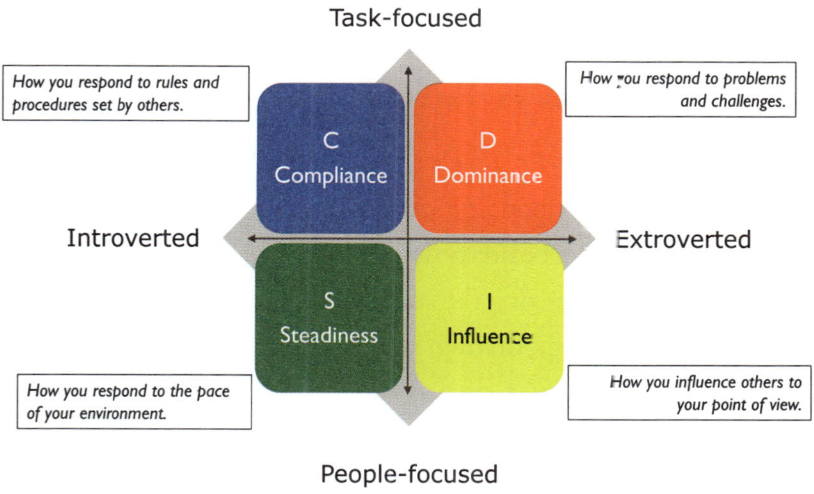


**Figure 1.1: The 4 DISC behavioural styles (Amended from source: Erikson, 2019).**

These 4 behavioural styles are situated along 2 dimensions. One dimension is whether you are task-focused or people-focused, and the other is whether you are introverted or extroverted. You as a leader exhibit all 4 behavioural styles in varying degrees of intensity. Based on the combination of these 4 styles, there are 5 team roles and many, many variables. Computerised reports that will tell you, for example, what your natural and adapted behavioural styles are, or offer detailed descriptions of your styles, strengths, and weaknesses and how you are being perceived by others, especially under medium pressure and high stress and more.

Successful leaders build on their natural tendencies where they come across strong and are aware of their weaknesses and development areas.

When it comes to weaknesses according to your natural tendencies, you need to select where you need to build leadership competencies to bridge the gap. Or occasionally find someone to fill the gap for you, although you still need to be aware of your weakness in that particular arena. Remember, there is no good or bad. The coin has two sides. Strengths and weaknesses are relative and subjective. They very much depend on the mandate you have and the role you need to fill.

For example, leaders with a high Dominance (Red) as their preferred style are very fast, responding quickly to the needs of the market (Figure 1.2). They can be pretty demanding. They're creative problem solvers and like challenging the status quo. They're very competitive and forward-thinking, driving changes in the future. They are quick decision-makers as time is money. The preferred keywords of this style are 'Win', 'Lead the field', 'Results', 'Now', 'New', and 'Challenge'. On the other hand, they can seem very pushy to some people (especially the Greens). They listen selectively and are so far ahead of the game that they need to remind themselves to slow down

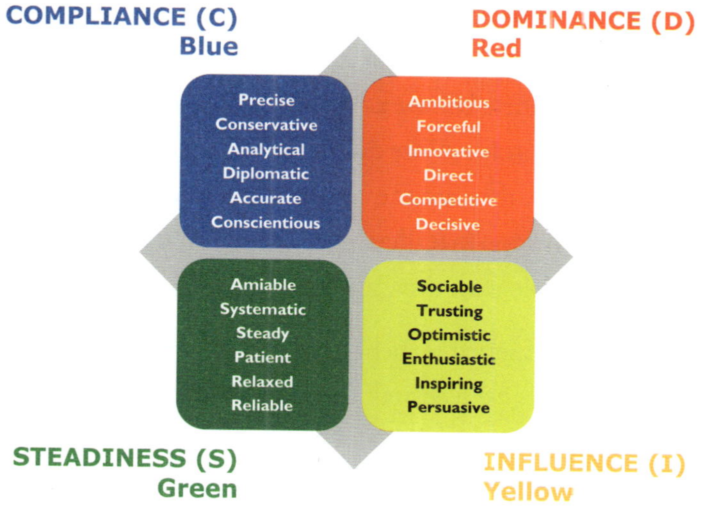


**Figure 1.2: Key descriptors of high-intensity DISC behavioural styles (Amended from source: Erikson, 2019).**

and wait for the others. They are straight to the point and see people through the lens of goals and tasks; therefore, they don't bother about connecting at a human-to-human level unless they can benefit from it. These leaders are not so good at noticing group dynamics and tend to neglect people's feelings and so on. When there is a profile, not only do the 4 styles speak differently based on the varying degrees of intensity but as they come together, it further tones the whole image. Apart from the natural styles in the profile, leaders also have adapted styles in the 4 behavioural factors. The adapted styles surface when they feel that there are either internal or external expectations for them to meet certain requirements for fulfilling the job. While the natural styles seldom change unless there are significant shifts and changes in life, the adapted styles are changeable, although this may require a lot of energy from the leader. Bear in mind that under stress and when leaders are tired, they fall back on their natural behaviour styles.

I combine motivators with DISC to see what the driving forces of the leaders are, and where their passion lies. These motivators not only tell us why leaders behave as they behave, but they further shade the picture of the profile. Why do they matter? Because they provide fuel for the leaders, they are the source of their energy. Finding their passion and motivation in leadership is a must; only then can they turn towards their people with drive and enthusiasm to inspire everyone.

DISC is about observable behaviours. When I profile leaders, I not only read and give feedback on their report based on their self-assessment, but I also teach them to learn this language and how they can apply it when they want to recognise the preferred and very noticeable styles of others. In addition, they can learn how to flex their own styles to others to improve the effectiveness of their communication and cooperation either within their leadership team or with external stakeholders. Although the natural tendencies are recognisable, be careful not to simplify them and put people into boxes using DISC. This tool is way more complex and colourful than mere boxes; we're human beings after all.

Use any diagnostic or self-assessment tool – be it DISC or something else – to raise your self-awareness and consciously build that knowledge into your own way of leadership. When your leadership is built on solid ground (i.e., your natural tendencies, strengths, and motivators) you will have a strong backbone with the heart to be REAL.

## A leader's projected image

The importance of perception, of how you are being perceived, is an inevitable part of leadership. Think of a situation when you have a leadership team meeting. You deliver a message of importance to the team members. Think about how that particular message could land differently for each member. We all have different lenses. This is how perception works. No matter what your intentions are, others may perceive you differently. It is easier to manage perceptions when you constantly bring your REAL SELF into the workplace instead of a fabricated image. You use your projected self, your so-called mask or your public persona for the world, when you don't show the real you, when you don't show your real feeling because you want to come across as a confident and powerful leader. Masking is when you put on a mask to meet real or perceived expectations and to please those around you. Being liked and accepted by others is a normal human desire, even for you as a leader.

Certain behavioural styles are more inclined to please others or seek approval or applause (high influence – the Yellows). They want to achieve this in such a way that they are ready to put some face on. They don't do it to manipulate, they do it to be accepted. This is where social media takes advantage of us as well.

What image you present, and show to the world matters a lot today, but it is all about projection, about projecting a perfect image. Social media tends to make us always talk about how successful we are, and very little about the not so successful elements of our lives. However, your imperfection makes you unique. It makes you depend on others; it makes you thrive more in teams instead of struggling alone. Misalignment between who you are, what you represent, and who you appear to be is a risky game.

I know a leader who made part-time female managers with children redundant saying that they did not meet the expectations of the firm because they couldn't invest extra working hours and go the extra mile due to their family commitment. (They did in fact meet the expectations, but not the extra ones.) A couple of years later, this same leader publicly endorsed the global HeForShe campaign supporting women in the workplace. This was a fake message from this leader and was absolutely misaligned between what he conveyed publicly and did internally.

If you say things to make yourself or the company look better while doing something different, these actions cannot be disguised for long; sooner or later, the truth will come to the surface in this highly transparent digital world and you will lose your credibility and then your followers. In this false reality, the importance of the image you represent is more important than who you are and what you stand for. This is sad. We all experience a lot of distortions. It shouldn't be like this; leadership shouldn't be built on this.

We live in an individualistic culture that values titles, positions, good looks, and achievements. Sometimes things only fall into place when you reach a milestone in your life but in between, it does not or may not look so fancy at all. Life is messy. You can easily become hostage to your position and title. These can be misleading. People in the organisation can see through your facade, behind your mask. Pretending, hiding your real emotions, and manipulating, intentionally or unintentionally, diminish trust and confidence simply because you are not being authentic. Maintaining an image takes a lot of energy. The more energy you spend on managing this image (or hiding behind such an image), the less energy you have to solve real problems, and the less resilient you become.

I have worked with many leaders on enhancing their visibility not only internally but externally, as well. Because of the noise of the digital space, you have to do more than you feel you should do. But be aware of the trap of visibility: in being overly visible, you can lose the connection to your real self and feed too much into your public persona. This is an ego game. If you let the environment feed your ego it will get out of control. It is the same as self-esteem. If your self-esteem depends on the feedback you receive, if you're on a high when you receive a lot of positive feedback and are shattered by negative feedback, then your self-esteem can become fragile. If your ego is being fed mostly by the likes and applause you get from your virtual or real audience, when you step away from your cheering crowds, for example, when you're between two positions, your ego will be bruised by the lack of cheerleading.

Never forget who you are while you are on your leadership journey. But since it is a journey, you are on your way to who you are becoming day by day. Every situation is a chance to demonstrate to the world who you really are, your TRUE SELF as a leader: The REAL LEADER.

The problem with masking and pretending is that you cannot fake it for a long time. Sooner or later, your mask will fall off and people will know who you really are. You will fail as a leader, and you will lose their trust. That said, there is a tiny bit of relevance and value in faking to appear strong, confident, competent, and successful.

**The 'fake it until you make it' dilemma**

---

### Leadership insights

"Although I may come across to you as a very confident leader, deep down inside, I am not that confident, really. I learnt an excellent technique: fake it until I make it. That's what I do. It works until my positive internal dialogues take over from my little gremlin who says things like:

I don't know everything! Should I say anything at all or just remain quiet and observe what is happening in the boardroom?

What if I say something stupid?

Am I good, unique, or interesting enough for this audience?

I am not influential and impactful!

I don't know all the details of this new trendy topic. I only know some; therefore, I shouldn't stand up on this stage or sit at this table to talk about this topic. I feel like an impostor."

---

## What is really happening here? What can you do about it?

1. It's easy to get trapped in a **cycle of negative belief,** which can manifest as self-fulfilling, negative prophecies with the help of your **self-saboteurs** who are equipped with well-constructed lies. Your internal (negative) messages have an enormous influence on your choices and the decisions you make. Watch out for these internal dialogues and work on your inner saboteurs.

2. Do you poorly **manage your own expectations?** How real is your expectation related to knowing everything about a subject, especially in this information-driven, data-overloaded digital world? As a leader, you don't need to know everything; you have a whole organisation to support you. But here is the question: How much information makes you credible in the eyes of your stakeholders? How or with whom can you bridge the gap? This can be difficult for those of you who have a high preference for details in the compliance behavioural style (High C from the DISC, the Blues).

3. You can make your life hell with lots of **assumptions** related to others and their expectations, and what they're thinking about you. There is a saying, "Your opinion of me is none of my business." And how true is that!

4. Do you live a **double life**, especially in the business world, masking your feelings, thoughts, and behaviours? Does doing this get you by, but cost you a lot of energy, to the detriment of your health (headaches, gallstones, digestive problems, cancer)? Are you disconnected from your authentic self, and no matter how successful you are, do you feel empty and unfulfilled? Learn about your natural and adapted behavioural styles and see how much you mask to achieve what you want.

But you have to fake it until you make it. Yes, it can work, as long as you never compromise your integrity. Or as social psychologist Amy Cuddy, puts it: "Don't fake it till you make it. Fake it till you become it. Do it enough until you actually become it, become of it and internalise it. Tiny tweaks can lead to big changes." Her research on body language reveals that we can change other people's perceptions — and even our own body chemistry — simply by changing our body positions. So not only change your inner dialogue but use power posing to raise your confidence: Fake it until you become it (Cuddy, 2012).

Meanwhile, do your homework. Work on yourself as a leader.

### Reflection points

- What negative inner talk keeps popping into your head?
- What lies are your saboteurs trying to tell you?
- How realistic are your expectations related to your goals and your dreams?
- What assumptions are you making about your most challenging situations and people?
- How aware are you of your own natural and adapted behavioural styles?

Why is this so important? Because if they, your people, your key stakeholders don't believe in you, they won't believe the messages you deliver, either.

## The authentic self as a leader

Who are you, really and truly? Are you building your leadership on your true self? Your authenticity very much depends on your self-awareness. Authentic leaders are REAL LEADERS. When you are authentic and true to yourself, you use a minimum level of energy. You don't have to think about how you should respond to things; you just respond naturally.

Based on my experience of profiling leaders, those leaders can be authentic and true to themselves whose natural behavioural styles are in line, or in fact the same as their adapted behavioural styles, a.k.a. masks. REAL LEADERS don't need to change their approach because of other people's expectations. They bring their authentic self to work. They are the same at work and at home as well.

"Authenticity means erasing the gap between what you firmly believe inside and what you reveal to the outside world" (Grant in Eggers–Barlow, 2019:77). Authenticity is when the image you project reflects who you really are (Figure 1.3). In his book, *An Everyone Culture*, Bob Kegan, a professor at Harvard School of Education, tells us that most working professionals have two full-time jobs: The first is their regular job (the one they are paid for) and the second, taking up an equal amount of time, is the additional job of managing their image and how they are perceived at work. This includes:

- Ensuring positive impressions
- Covering up their inadequacies
- Managing other people's impressions
- Showing themselves to their best advantage
- Avoiding negative impressions
- Playing politics
- Hiding weaknesses
- Hiding uncertainties (Eggers and Barlow, 2019:77–78).

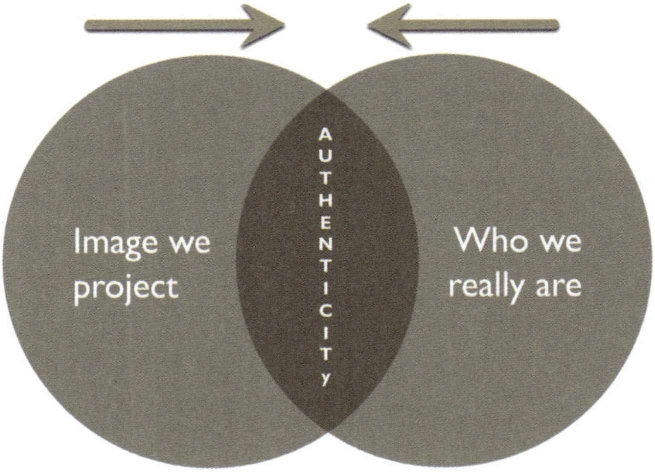


**Figure 1.3: Authenticity in the overlap (Eggers and Barlow, 2019:77).**

Authenticity is the alignment of music (voice), dance (body language), words (verbal communication) with your head and heart (thinking and feeling) or to put it in another way, the alignment of head, heart, mouth, and feet; thinking, feeling, saying, and doing the same thing consistently. Who are you on good days and who are you in times of adversity? Are you the same?

What stops you from being authentic? Are you afraid of being exposed, of being unworthy, of not being good enough? Are you afraid of losing a perception you pride yourself on?

You have complete authority over who you are as a leader and the story you tell about yourself to the world.

### Reflection points

Your authentic self:

- Who are you when you have no fear of judgement, when you don't want to please others, meet expectations, both real and perceived? Who are you really?
- What kind of leader are you?
- What kind of leader do you want to become?
- How do who you are as a leader and what you believe in influence the type of organisation you are part of and want to create?

This does not happen accidentally. It is a conscious decision.

## The value-driven leader

What are your key values? What values do you hold dear? Being a REAL LEADER also means being an authentic, value-driven leader, which is about being fully aware of what your non-negotiables are. What lines or boundaries do you refuse to cross? What do you stand for? These are big questions, I know. Your first answer is sometimes too abstract. But they are truly the foundation of your being a REAL LEADER, of living your life from the inside out. If you live your life with integrity, it means you live your life following your personal values. If you live from the outside in, then your environment dictates who you are, which can easily distort the picture of the real you.

What do you fall back on when there is too much compromise to make? How far would you go for success? Don't think of illegal decisions, think of all the everyday compromises that erode your values slowly, day by day. One day you wake up and hardly recognise the person you have become. You start blaming the management, the corporate world, the government, your customers, but you never consider that it was you who made all those choices. It was your decision; it is you who let yourself down. You become unguarded and extremely fragile.

Since everything starts with leadership, you must embrace and respect your own values first. You as a leader can respect and honour other people's values only after you have done it for yourself first.

Your values are built on your heritage, where you come from, and who you are, but also on who you want to become in the future. How can your values be future-focused? Is it possible? Values are always personal. They are the foundation of the quality of life you decide to live, and the quality of leader you are and want to become. When your values are suppressed and not honoured, you pay the price.

An executive client of mine at a huge multinational corporation had to fulfil many roles at the same time. It took so much energy from him, that he was pushed to the limit of burning out. He got sick and had to go to the hospital for surgery. Now I know we can't say for sure that he got sick because of the enormous workload and energy he put into his job without any time and space for recovery; nevertheless, it made him realise he couldn't go on like that. Many leaders are strong, ambitious, and driven. They are not afraid of the extra effort required and unfortunately, they tend to miss the early signs that they're pushing too far until it is too late.

Honouring your personal, social, and moral values helps keep yourself in balance and on track in your life as a whole. Be a value-driven leader because it has its rewards at the system level as well. When you are clear about your values, when you live by them and cherish them, you start looking at people through the lens of values. What are their values? How can you add value to them? What do you value in them? There's a greater alignment with your inner self, which will help you connect with and inspire others much more.

### *Values exercise*

What are your values? What do you stand for? What are the 5 most important things both in your professional and personal life, because you don't live your life in separate compartments?

**Select the 5 most important values for you:**

| | | | |
|---|---|---|---|
| Family | Freedom | Security | Loyalty |
| Intelligence | Connection | Creativity | Humanity |
| Success | Respect | Innovation | Diversity |
| Generosity | Integrity | Finesse | Love |
| Openness | Religion | Order | Advancement |
| Respect | Joy | Playfulness | Forgiveness |
| Excitement | Change | Goodness | Passion |
| Faith | Wisdom | Beauty | Caring |
| Personal Development | Honesty | Adventure | Kindness |
| Teamwork | Career | Hope | Learning |
| Excellence | Innovation | Quality | Commonality |

| | | | |
|---|---|---|---|
| Contribution | Spiritualism | Strength | Entertainment |
| Wealth | Speed | Power | Affection |
| Cooperation | Love of Career | Relationship | Support |
| Pride in Your Work | Clarity | Impact | Charisma |
| Humour | Leadership | Renewal | Communication |
| Truth | Contentment | Friendship | Courage |
| Balance | Compassion | Fitness | Professionalism |
| Relationship | Knowledge | Patience | Influence |
| Prosperity | Well-being | Finances | Gratitude |
| Grace | Endurance | Facilitation | Effectiveness |
| Fun | Reputation | Justice | Appreciation |
| Willingness | Intuition | Giving People a Chance | Peace |
| Forgiveness | Self-Respect | Abundance | Reciprocity |
| Enjoyment | Entrepreneur-ship | Happiness | Harmony |
| Other.................. | ............................ | ............................ | ............................ |

### Reflection points

- How did you honour your values this week?
- How will you honour your values next week?
- What rituals must you implement to cherish your values?
- What are the threats that make you compromise your values every single day?
- What lines or boundaries will you refuse to cross?

In summary, authenticity includes who you really are, what your values are, what your natural behavioural tendencies are, and what your motivators, your driving forces (the sources of your passion) are. There is one more aspect of being a REAL LEADER we need to unfold: your integrity (your moral compass, your impact, your intention).

## Integrity

### Your moral compass

The compass itself is a relatively simple device yet when we talk about our moral compass it gets more and more complicated. In my approach, your moral compass consists of your beliefs (both positive and negative) that influence your filters of how you see the world, and your personal, moral, and social values. Your moral compass appears in your everyday life like a right and wrong dilemma, which is quite a challenge and in fact, can be quite contradictory in today's complex business environment.

Do you have rituals of checking whether you are still in line with your compass, whether you are improving and continuously learning along the road?

To keep your integrity as a leader you can focus on 3 elements and keep checking yourself against them. Check the ethical side of your decisions and what consequences they entail. Check what impact your words and actions have, or don't have, on others, organisations, results, and society. Check your intention and whether your intention is in line with your action and your impact.

### The ethical side of your decisions

You need brutal honesty and courage to do the right thing. But what is the right thing?

Don't look at frameworks as tick-box exercises. Don't simply work through all the elements to tick all the boxes and then expect to come out with the right answer. This is all wrong. Real-life leadership today is full of ambiguity and paradoxes; grey areas abound. No framework can ever account for every possibility you might face. And this applies even more so to ethics. Then what are frameworks for? They are still useful to help guide your thinking. But simply checking the items off the list is not enough. You need to look inside yourself and check your moral compass regularly as well.

### The flat white framework

The flat white framework is a simple framework for making ethical decisions. Leaders often have very little time to gather data or go through all the data at their disposal to reach the best decision.

So, you have to go with what you've got. You only need a little time to reflect and go through all the questions. Don't labour the process. Be quick and concise in your answers and as far as possible, take a holistic view. Do this exercise in the morning to cover Maryam Kouchaki and Isaac H. Smith's 'morning morality effect'. According to Kouchaki and Smith (2013), evidence suggests that people are more likely to make ethical decisions early in the day.

Witzel (2019:184) poses 11 questions in the flat white framework to consider and help you reach ethical decisions:

1. What do you know about this situation, and what don't you know?
2. What are your own loyalties and biases? What might influence your decision one way or the other?
3. What stakeholder groups are involved, and how?
4. What options are open to you? If they are unsatisfactory, can other options be created?
5. What issues of right and wrong are involved?
6. What are the good and bad consequences of these options?
7. Which option would yield the result that is most fair and equitable?
8. What do you want?
9. In your heart, what do you feel you should do?
10. Can you live with the consequences of your actions?
11. What will you do if it turns out your decision is wrong?

### *Your impact as a leader*

How you show up at work as a leader (connected or disconnected, energised or tired, real or pretending) impacts the people around you, the people you lead.

Also, what you do or don't do and what you say or don't say have an impact on others, on your teams, on your organisation, on key stakeholders, on results, and on the community.

Is this the impact you want to make? Is this the legacy, the footprint you want to leave behind?

When you as a leader don't say anything, when you turn away, when you close your eyes, when you accept mediocre work without accountability, it is not only about honesty. It requires courage to speak up and act on it. This is why you are a leader. Doing the right thing often comes with a high cost, but the very moment you let it be, you ignore your moral compass. When you ignore who and what you stand for, you are no longer a leader.

Whatever you do or don't do and whatever you say or don't say - how does this impact others, your family, your organisation, your decisions, results, etc? Keep asking yourself!

## Checking intention vs impact as a leader

You need to be clear about your intention as a leader. It is so easy to judge others by their behaviours and ourselves by our intentions. The most challenging part is to be consistent; ensure that your intentions and actions align. According to Wiseman (2017), leaders have multiplier and diminisher tendencies. The tricky diminisher tendencies are the ones that are accidentally done.

### *Accidental diminishers*

Accidental diminishers (Wiseman, 2017) are well-intended leaders who think they are doing a great job at leading, but they are only vaguely aware or completely unaware of their negative impact on their environment. All leaders have accidental diminisher moments. You, too.

The secret is knowing what your vulnerabilities are, spotting them in action, and turning those situations into multiplier moments. You can increase your awareness as a leader by identifying your own diminisher tendencies. Which of these resonate with you?

#### Idea Guys Leaders

- **Intention:** This type of leader is a very creative, innovative thinker, an ideas generator, who loves an idea-rich environment. They throw ideas in to stimulate ideas in others. (High I, the Yellows)
- **Impact:** They tend to overwhelm others, who shut down or spend time chasing ideas after ideas until they eventually give up. They not only stop acting but also stop trying to come up with their own ideas. So, it is easy to get ideas-lazy around people who are ideas-rich.

#### Always On Leaders

- **Intention:** Dynamic, charismatic leaders who are always engaged, always present, and always have something to say. Their intention is to create contagious energy. (High D, the Reds)
- **Impact:** They use up all the space, and drain all the energy as they consume all the available oxygen around them while others suffocate. When a leader is always on, everyone else is always off.

## Rescuer Leaders

- **Intention:** Good leaders with noble intentions who want to ensure people are successful and protect their reputation. These leaders, more often than not, lend a hand, resolve a problem, and help people across the finish line. (High S, the Greens)
- **Impact:** People become dependent and helpless, which weakens their reputation. Instead of feeling successful, employees experience frustration and depleted confidence. They are not learning and developing.

## Pacesetter Leaders

- **Intention:** Achievement-oriented leaders who lead by example and set a high standard for quality or pace. They exemplify the values of the organisation, such as quality, customer service, and innovation. (Mixture of High D & C, a mixture of the Reds and the Blues.)
- **Impact:** Others become spectators or give up when they can't keep up. These leaders tend to get out ahead of their team thinking that other people will follow, but actually, people tend to slow down. And when they lead by setting the pace, they end up creating more spectators than followers.

## Rapid Responder Leaders

- **Intention:** Prize agility and fast turnaround to keep their organisation moving fast and respond to their stakeholders quickly. They are quick to respond, troubleshoot problems, and make fast micro-decisions. When they see a problem, they solve it. Emails don't last long in their inbox. They open, read, and resolve them immediately. (High D, the Reds)

- **Impact:** Their organisation moves slowly because of the traffic jam of too many decisions or changes coming from the leader. And people tend to defer to them and then wait.

## Optimist Leaders

- **Intention:** Always see possibilities and believe that most problems can be tackled with hard work and the right mindset. They are 'glass half full' kind of people. And their intentions are to create the belief that the team can do it. (High I, the Yellows)
- **Impact:** People think they undervalue the struggle the team is experiencing and don't appreciate their hard-fought learning and work. Employees may wonder if these leaders have lost their connection to reality, causing people to play it safe or not want to attempt hard things.

## Protector Leaders

- **Intention:** 'Banyan tree' leaders, who shield their staff from the hazards of corporate life and keep people safe from political forces in the organisation. (High S, the Greens)
- **Impact:** Unfortunately, nothing grows under a Banyan tree, so these leaders prevent people from learning about hardship and taking full responsibility. They don't learn to fend for themselves.

## Strategist Leaders

- **Intention:** Big thinkers who cast a compelling vision of the future to move beyond the status quo. They show the team a better place, a destination worth striving for and sell it with evangelical zeal. (High D, the Reds)
- **Impact:** They paint such a big vision that other people don't have to do the big thinking and they become short-sighted,

often small thinking. These leaders also don't give space for their people to think through the challenges themselves and develop the intellectual muscle needed to make a vision a reality.

## Perfectionist Leaders

- **Intention:** Helping people produce outstanding work they are proud of, they go beyond setting a high standard for others to follow (as the Pacesetter) and want everyone around them to have the same satisfaction of getting it just exactly right. (High C, the Blues)
- **Impact:** People feel criticised, become disheartened, and stop trying. People feel no matter how hard they try nothing is ever good enough.

### Reflection points

- Can you identify your areas of vulnerability? Do you know your leadership blind spots?
- Which of these accidental diminisher tendencies can you recognise in your leadership practice? We all have accidental diminisher moments.
- Remember the first learning point here is to be able to recognise where you accidentally diminish your people's efforts and contributions, even if your intentions are positive.
- How can you turn the volume down in order not to have a diminishing impact?
- What else can you do to change the impact of your naturally positive intention? How can you work around it?

## A high-level introduction to the CRAFT model

What is your CRAFT? What makes you a unique and powerful leader? Being powerful partly comes from connecting to and reclaiming your true nature, in other words, being in line with your REAL SELF as a leader. But it also means to be future-reading and future-proof as a leader.

How ready are you for future leadership challenges?

Define your leadership. How and in what way do you want to be CRAFTed? What is your CRAFT as a leader?

**C – CREATIVITY** What does creativity mean for you? How can it be captured in your organisation? What is your role in it?

**R – RESILIENCE** What does resilience mean for you? What does a resilient leader/organisation look like? How can you become more resilient?

**A – AGILITY** Why does agility matter so much today? How do you demonstrate agility as a leader? How can you develop agility in the most fundamental way?

**F – FOCUS** How hard or easy do you find it to focus as a leader? What challenges do you face when you are setting the focus and priorities for yourself and for your organisation? What do you need to consider and implement to master this quality?

**T – TRUST** What makes you a trustworthy leader? How can you build one-on-one trust? How can you create greater trust within and without your organisation?

Where are you strong in the 5 CRAFT Leadership qualities explored in this book and where do you need to further sharpen yourself? Read to the end to find out.

CRAFT Leadership is an integrated model (Figure 1.4). It is sometimes difficult to separate each quality in practice as they may appear together and influence one another. And everything starts with yourself as the REAL LEADER.

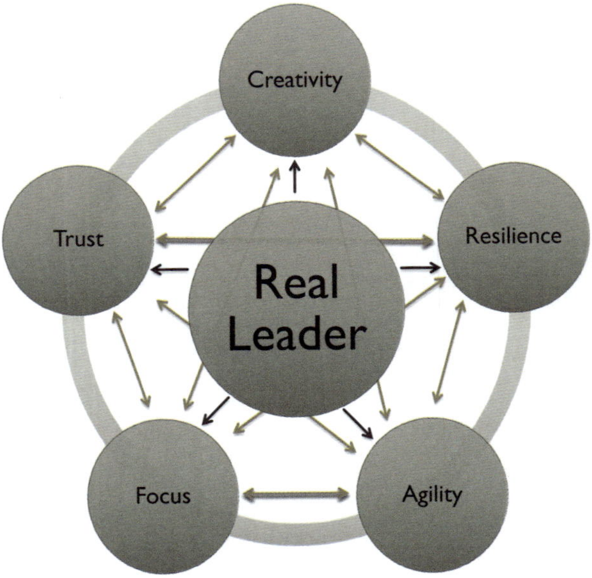


**Figure 1.4: CRAFT Leadership (Source: Author's own).**

Let's start with the first of the 5 CRAFT Leadership qualities: CREATIVITY.

# CHAPTER II

## C is for CREATIVITY and CREATE

"Creativity is as individual as a snowflake."

(Jeff Benjamin, cited in Nixon, 2020)

### The business context of CREATIVITY for today and tomorrow

Why does creativity matter so much? In today's dynamic, competitive, and increasingly connected global world, creativity and innovation are a must to get ahead of the competitors and to survive and thrive at the same time. No enterprise can be successful without differentiating business ideas and solutions. Creativity and innovation are especially important when the market in a given sector is overcrowded. Creativity is needed to anticipate and prepare for the future. Leaders need to see more "more" and more "before" as John C. Maxwell (2018) puts it.

You need to see possibilities when others don't. You need to give and facilitate answers to complex challenges. You need to connect the unconnected dots and you can't achieve this without thinking creatively, out of the box. An excessive focus on striving towards efficiency can kill creativity, even though creativity is also a kind of productivity game, especially when it turns into innovation. Therefore, CREATIVITY and CREATE are destined to be the C in CRAFT Leadership. As a leader, you not only have responsibility for developing your own creativity and improving yourself as a creator, but also you are responsible for creating an environment in your organisation where creativity has its place and role. You must help your people unleash their creativity, too.

The world around us is changing at an exponential rate. Globalisation and technical advancements, with their effects, are two of the main global forces that impact creativity and innovation since both are opening up the world to us. Both are enablers and disruptors at the same time; they shepherd or sometimes push organisations towards creativity and innovation. Creativity is a great accelerant and applies to organisations of any type, in any sector.

This is great because if you are entrepreneurial, innovative, and creative as an individual or as an organisation, what you have here is an exploding universe of opportunities. Loads of opportunities are not just happening but expanding constantly in front of you. All you have to do is to scan the horizon, grab hold of new things, and you are off on your next innovation journey. However, we individuals don't have the mental capacity to keep up with all these changes; although we have great potential, we don't optimise it. We are good, but not good enough for the explosion of exponential change that is happening around us. As human beings, we are primarily backwards-looking individuals, i.e., we make sense of our world by looking backwards. Most of the time we solve problems from our experience and knowledge. We filter through those lenses and select what is relevant today and apply it. This determines our future behaviour.

## Our past has a profound effect on our future

At a workshop by David J. Hall, Founder of Idea Center (2017), I learnt that our past can limit our future. We can improve over time, but unfortunately at a much slower rate, so we create an ever-increasing gap between what is and what might be. If there is a problem we instinctively look back before we decide what to do next. This traps us in our 'what is' circle, where we use our conventional and traditional thinking most of the time. We tend to consider only those ideas that are within this circle and dismiss those beyond it.

Decisions in established organisations are still made with this backwards-looking perception. A typical example of this is setting the annual budget. It is still prepared based on past results mostly as a benchmark; there is very little focus on the future potential of the organisation. Therefore, creativity is an essential asset to innovate, navigate complexity, and thrive in today's world.

You might recognise these signals and potential blind spots when your organisation lags in this field (Nixon, 2020):

- When organisations get larger and more focused on risk management, they easily fall into the trap of what Natalie Nixon (2020) calls "the tyranny of no". They solve for 'no' instead of for 'yes.' Solving for 'yes' is the foundation of creativity.
- When organisations find themselves at the head of the group, the "too big to fail" assumption and the superiority complex emerge. But where does that mindset come from? These firms don't innovate quickly enough. They get complacent and stuck. Just think of Kodak.

## Anecdote 1. What happened with Kodak?

In the 1970s, Kodak was a dominant player in the photographic industry. They had cheap cameras. They made the most of their revenue by selling films. Surprisingly, Kodak invented the digital camera. However, the board dismissed the idea because no film was needed. And most of their revenue at that time came from selling films. Kodak cancelled all research and development and all marketing activities; they said it would be suicidal to introduce a product to the market that did not need film because they were a film-based organisation, and all their success was driven by film. They looked backwards and decided accordingly. The competition picked up their idea and succeeded, while Kodak filed for bankruptcy. So, Kodak is history. 'Innovate or die' is a familiar catchphrase in the business world. Perhaps it would be better formulated as 'innovate or bleed to death very slowly' as happened with Kodak. When leaders make decisions on experience and follow conservative and traditional thinking, they pay a high price. And it wasn't just Kodak. What about BlackBerry? Or Nokia?

**Key pain points** in creativity are the lack of space, time, and resources within the organisation. Creativity has many facets; leaders tend to mobilise only a few of them. Most leaders and people think of creativity as brainstorming. There are also opposing forces within organisations that can kill creativity, for example, two productivity games: efficiency vs innovation. A leader's inability and lack of courage to see the greater business potential and the keys to a competitive edge in the very detail of creativity undermine the power of it; therefore, it ends up at the bottom of the organisation's list of priorities.

The good news from Maya Angelou (2014) is that "You can't use up creativity. The more you use, the more you have."

Let's explore some theories behind creativity, the meaning and definition of creativity, its key components, and what today's leaders say about the need, place, and demonstration of creativity within their organisations. We'll then move on to how to master this leadership quality through the following 6 areas:

- The CREATIVITY cocktail (3 ingredients)
- CREATIVITY and continuous improvement
- CREATIVITY and innovation
- CREATIVITY and strategy
- The Leader as a CREATOR
- CRAFTing the future

## The theory of CREATIVITY

According to the Cambridge dictionary: "Creativity is the ability to produce or use original and unusual ideas, or to make something new or imaginative."

Nixon (2020) defines creativity as "the ability to toggle between wonder and rigour in order to solve problems and deliver novel value. And I see inquiry, improvisation, and intuition as the practices that increase those capacities."

It is important to make a differentiation between CREATIVITY (the noun) and TO CREATE (the verb). Both play a significant role in leadership.

As a leader, your role is not only to enhance creativity within your organisation but also to create the right conditions for your organisation and your people to thrive.

Let's start with creativity. Guilford (1950) talks about creativity being manifested in divergent thinking. Divergent thinking allows us to approach a problem from multiple perspectives or to connect elements that are usually considered independent or incompatible. Together with Torrance (Guilford and Torrance in Fodor, 2007), he developed 10 components of creativity:

- **Fluence:** The fluidity of mental activity by generating large numbers of ideas with ease and speed.
- **Flexibility:** The ability to adapt to changing needs, by using a variety of approaches, as a result of creating different ideas and solution techniques.
- **Originality:** Unexpected, novel ideas and thoughts that can give very different answers to problems.
- **Sensitivity:** Creative individuals recognise problems that others cannot see or interpret as an average phenomenon.
- **Elaboration:** The need and effort to elaborate the details and organise information in a structured way.
- **Re-definition:** The re-organisation and interpretation of intellectual structures, objects, and details are detected differently than usual. Because of this different perception, the object or part of it is used in new, hitherto unknown ways.
- **Synthesisation:** Creative people organise their thoughts into larger and more complete sets of thoughts and through this, they can easily embrace complexity.

- **Analysis:** Syntheses created by others (comparisons, ready-made structures) are not accepted. The structure is re-analysed to create a new one.
- **Complexity:** Creative people can work with many interconnected ideas. The relationships are also interpreted in a different way.
- **Evaluation:** Creative people are critical and can easily determine the value of new ideas.

Going through this list you may wonder how these can all be in one person, especially considering the business context in which creativity is needed. Tackling business creativity along with innovation can only be achieved in teams. Therefore, your role as a leader to present and apply these components in a team and organisation is a complex task.

## What creativity means to the leaders I interviewed

As a leader, your role is to see where the organisation can and can't be creative and then to create a trusted and respectful supportive environment to make it happen. This requires an entrepreneurial mindset, i.e., being able to think outside the box and getting out of your comfort zone to come up with solutions and ideas that are not so obvious in the specific business context. Break the habit of doing the same thing time after time. Networks to be inspired by are very different. Look for people who bring the unexpected into the conversation, and perspectives not yet considered. You need to recognise when you (as an individual and as an organisation) move into copy-paste and break this pattern. Add new to the old. Reinvent the old. Create something new from what is old. Create something completely new. Ask big, open questions sometimes or on the contrary, ask very specific probing questions. Create an ideas-generation culture similar to a feedback culture. To achieve this, tear down the walls and eliminate the fear. Take a current business situation, it could be a market-, customer- or employee-related issue, and find the best answer to it, preferably as unique an answer as possible. Encourage people to think, to innovate, to engrave possibility-thinking under their skin. Brainstorming sessions and ideas coming from the bottom up are worthless if there is no feedback on what will happen to the ideas they generate. Your stakeholder group for your company could be so diverse and complex, that finding a common path (a win-win for everyone) will also require creativity. Creativity means being able to renew yourself and your organisation from time to time to stay relevant and competitive.

## Anecdote 2. How to capture creativity in an organisation

One multinational technology company launched a programme primarily focusing on fresh graduates while also encouraging teams to generate ideas. Every 6 months, the graduates at the company come up with a project idea and put together a proposal for a chosen business result or industry-related issue. They can also choose to improve a particular internal process. There are generally 6 to 8 projects/programmes running at any one time. Each project is led by a group of 2 or 3 people as programme owners (with a mix of fresh and more experienced colleagues). They spend 1 or 2 days a week on it, which is quite a lot if you think about it. They have to present the proposal to the board and, if the board finds it worth pursuing, they can get working hours approved so that they can carry on working on their ideas and projects. Then the leaders consider the time spent on idea generation as client-paid hours. Some of the projects are already in the second phase as they got a green light from the board while the rest are new ideas and projects.

The second phase can consist of further developing and testing or implementing the idea, or taking the idea to a client to assess its feasibility and business potential. So far, they have sold one idea created like this to a big client. This is how they plant the seed of creativity and innovation in the organisation – by starting with fresh graduates and supporting them with experienced colleagues.

Another example involves a sales division of a bank. They use gamification as a tool to awaken the enthusiastic and creative inner child in the sales forces by bringing playfulness and humour into very competitive sales target areas. Different themes have been introduced as part of various sales campaigns. For example, during the European Football Championship, they launched a team competition and said there must be someone in every place on the field for a winning team, like in football. While not everyone can be a striker, others may pass the ball to the striker to score a goal. This not only stirred the competition in the division but encouraged teamwork.

Yet another example of using creativity was a campaign based on an old Hungarian King Matthias tale called "There was once a dog fair in Buda." Although the original idea came from the leader, who happened to be very creative, the management team further developed it. They picked this ancient tale because of the dogs. Dogs symbolise loyalty. They are (wo)man's best friends. People generally have positive feelings about them. Therefore, this gamification helped many salespeople to let go of their negative feelings about certain products. This initiative aimed to bridge the efficiency requirements of the company with real value creation and needs-based selling and eliminate an emerging bad tendency within the division where people started offering only the more expensive products to customers, neglecting the cheaper but still relevant and important solutions in the sales. The game was about selling more products from the company's portfolio within a customer call. They had different flags created for each dog. They not only linked different products with different types of dogs, like a sausage dog for selling a single product, but they also added quantity to the sale. For example, if they sold 4 products in a call, they'd get a Great Dane flag. Whoever collected the most flags with bigger dogs was the winner. As a result, the number of sales per call increased from an average of 1.3 to 4 in many cases and employees learnt to better explore the customer's needs in one call. This creative idea generated not only fun, energy, and motivation, but again planted the seed of creativity within the whole division. This leader truly believes that people are Homo Ludens (i.e., man the player).

## Leadership insights

"We insist on what is tried. Maintaining stability, avoiding instability, or striving for stability are natural human needs that can be achieved with solutions and ways of operation that are tested. Most organisations think from the inside out instead of thinking from the outside in. We should look more from the outside, reflect on our observations, and then think and create something new. A castle cannot be taken in frontally; it must be gone around or approached from underneath. To have a new perspective, we have to come out of our castle. This cannot be achieved without curiosity. It starts with a true assessment of ourselves, where we may realise that we often or rather most of the time work in our comfort zone, in our castles."

"I am a creative leader; I have a lot of ideas. Sadly, there is an empty space behind me. So far, I've always looked for and hired reliable people with a controlling mindset and approach. But unfortunately, these types of leaders have a hard time being creative. I'm not saying that those who are creative aren't reliable, but they're very different types of people. This is a difficult balancing act."

"One of the modern ethical dilemmas related to creativity and creation is: Should creativity be limited? Are robotics and automation for people or against people? How long do they serve people? Who is responsible for the actions of robots? Is value creation for a limited number of people (e.g., shareholders) or for a whole community (considering greater impacts)? If we say this is for the greater good of the future of humankind but we sacrifice people's livelihood here and now, is it ok then?"

## The CREATIVITY cocktail – How to develop CREATIVITY

When we talk about developing creativity, we not only refer to your own creativity as a leader but also what you can do to enhance the creativity of your organisation.

How often have you heard people say, "Oh, I'm not a creative type"? Or perhaps you've thought this yourself. This is a false thought. We, humans, are hardwired to be creative in one way or the other. Even analytical people have what it takes to be creative to some extent. Creativity is a combination of muscles that can be developed. Or as I like to say, creativity is a cocktail that contains specific ingredients, some of which you may have, others that can be bought, borrowed, or grown (Figure 2.1).

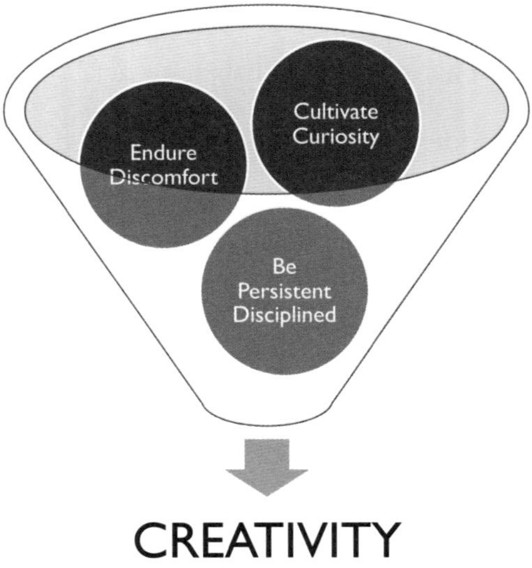


**Figure 2.1: The CREATIVITY Cocktail (Source: Author's own).**

## Ingredient #1 - Ignite and cultivate curiosity within yourself and in your teams

Children are born with an abundance of curiosity that fades as they grow into adults. Children are brilliant when it comes to creativity; in fact, 98% of children at the age of 4 are creative geniuses. At the age of 10, this number drops to 30%. At the age of 15, only 12% of them are brilliant at creativity. Isn't it sad how our education system and our full 'cognitive' filing cabinet can destroy our creativity! This is, I am afraid, a natural process of growing up (Venkatraman, 2018).

How can you tap into your inner child and how can you create an environment where your people can tap into their inner child, too?

**Table 2.1: Ingredient #1 - Ignite and cultivate curiosity within yourself and in your teams**

| Ingredients of igniting and cultivating curiosity | How to build this leadership muscle |
|---|---|
| **Observe and notice** things around you internally and externally, in the here and now and from a distance. | You must first slow down in order to speed up. Allow yourself to step out of your doing mode and observe what is happening in your leadership team. For example, put a topic on the table and just watch how people talk. Notice the energy flows in the room. See how they non-verbally respond to each other, etc.<br><br>Take a helicopter or meta-view to distance yourself (imagine you are in a helicopter taking off). What can you see from a distance? What patterns can you notice that you missed when you were in the middle of the situation? What impact do your actions have on the organisation, on its results? |
| **Be inquisitive** by asking many good, probing, insightful questions.<br><br>Some questions may appear to be inadequate and even silly in the given situation; nevertheless, they can help you make a real shift.<br><br>The thinking process should be led and facilitated by questions. | Ask not only open questions but 'What if....', 'Why', 'Why not', and 'How....' types of questions as well. For example, what if we partnered with our biggest competitor? What is trying to emerge here?<br><br>Reflect on your 'as is' operation: How often do you ask questions during the workday? What sort of questions do you ask?<br><br>Prepare for meetings by writing down as many questions as you can related to the topic. Your last few questions could be 'What am I missing here?' 'What am I not seeing here?' 'What questions am I avoiding here?' |

| Ingredients of igniting and cultivating curiosity | How to build this leadership muscle |
|---|---|
| **Be passionate and enthusiastic**. | Enthusiasm and passion are fuel. They create energy and sparks not just within but around you, as well. And they're contagious. But they have to be authentic. You cannot fake them, because it will show through. This is about you, how you choose to be present as a REAL LEADER.<br><br>What do you passionately like about what you do as a leader? How can you amplify it? What is most exciting about a specific topic for you? |
| **Listen to your intuition,** what your gut feeling tells you. | Intuition is the connection between the heart and the mind and is grounded in your gut. It is internal wisdom, unconscious pattern recognition, and insight for decision-making. To tap into your intuition, you have to slow down and create distance between yourself and the reality or the topic at hand. It also requires courage to listen to your intuition, let alone have your intuition influence your decision. Ask yourself "What is my gut feeling here?"<br><br>Even after you get that intuitive nudge, you might have a natural tendency to hold back, to analyse it, to check and see if it is right, or if this is the right time to say something. But regarding intuition, the most powerful moment is always the first one. You have to blurt it out and phrase it like 'I wonder if.....', 'I have a hunch that......' 'My intuition tells me...' 'I'm not sure what the right words are here, but it's something like...' etc. |

| Ingredients of igniting and cultivating curiosity | How to build this leadership muscle |
|---|---|
| **Be a perpetual learner.** | Be open and willing to learn new things. Your career decline will start when you stop learning. Make learning intentional, an everyday routine. Keep a reflection/learning notebook where you jot down your thoughts and feelings at the end of each day. This could be 15 minutes with wine/beer/tea. There is no effective leadership without conscious leadership and there is no conscious leadership without reflection and learning. |
| **Be eager to challenge the status quo,** the tried and tested ways. | Encourage your people at every level and in every part of the business to ask questions, challenge the status quo and even challenge you as a leader with new ideas and new ways of thinking.<br><br>It is easier said than done, especially when you as a leader or the way you lead is being challenged by someone decades younger than you. |
| **Use your imagination,** be insightful, genuine, and naive. | Take the edge off seriousness with playfulness. Use techniques that help you and your team tap into your inner child. This can only be achieved if you create a safe environment. Explore the idea with a metaphor that may pop up during the discussion. Or buy a magazine from a field you have no interest in. Browse through it and identify at least 3 approaches or ideas that could be useful metaphors for the challenge at hand.<br><br>Exercise wonder, pausing, dreaming, and daring to do some blue-sky thinking. What would you do if you had all the money, time, and resources in the world?<br><br>Allow yourself to daydream |

| Ingredients of igniting and cultivating curiosity | How to build this leadership muscle |
|---|---|
| **Connect the dots,** especially ones that have never been connected. | The best exercise I can recommend here is one we talk about later in this chapter: 'Reconstruct market boundaries – the 6 paths framework' (Kim and Mabourgne, 2005; 2017).<br><br>Internally ask yourself what would happen, if you connected those people who have never been connected? In what way should you connect them? What are the potentials of these new connections? What are the risks?<br><br>Interestingly, it's like an oxymoron: matching things that don't match and making a new definition or thought. New things are born. |
| **Be open to different perspectives and ideas.** Get out of your own head. | In your leadership team, ask each team member to represent key stakeholders. Explore their thoughts, actions, feelings, and intentions on the topic at hand. They should place themselves in the shoes of those stakeholders and bring everything to the table through their lenses and their behaviours.<br><br>Who is the thirteenth fairy, the one you always fail to invite and who may have an enormous impact on your business? Who have you missed from your stakeholder list?<br><br>Invite someone very unusual to the leadership table. For example, an intern who just joined the company or someone from outside the organisation. |

| Ingredients of igniting and cultivating curiosity | How to build this leadership muscle |
|---|---|
| **Improvise** by building on the ideas of others without constraints and judgement with the help of being here and now. | Build on each other's ideas by using the 'Yes, and' technique within your team. Set a rule that everyone has to discuss the topic by starting their sentence with 'Yes, and' for the whole meeting.<br><br>Improvisation does not mean doing whatever you feel like; it has rules and fluid structures that help you embrace mistakes, observe, and adapt. Examples of great improvisation can be found in jazz, comedy, excellent sales/customer service experiences, and scientific experimentation. Use minimal structures to maximise flexibility like the jazz musicians (Nixon, 2020). |

## Ingredient #2 – Endure discomfort

You need not only to bear the pain and frustration but to learn to appreciate the value of sitting with the discomfort that comes from the ambiguity and uncertainty of the idea-creation process. It sometimes means building on mistakes like the creation of Post-its by 3M (Nixon, 2020). Sitting with discomfort in the unknown while generating new ideas requires endurance from anyone.

**Table 2.2: Ingredient #2 – Endure discomfort**

| Ingredients of enduring discomfort | How to build this leadership muscle |
|---|---|
| **Break out of and reconstruct boundaries.** | We are habitually territorial creatures, who like boundaries because they give us security and the sense of belonging to somewhere and someone.<br><br>The simplest way to train yourself to reconstruct boundaries and break habits is to go to work a different way every day for two weeks.<br><br>In the subsection of CREATIVITY and strategy, you will see how you can reconstruct market boundaries using a framework. |
| **Tap into and stay in the unknown.** | Don't be afraid of being wrong. Accept you are no longer the one who knows everything. But you are the one who leads. You're the role model for exploring areas that are unknown or unusual. This requires a lot of courage from leaders.<br><br>Admitting that you are both an explorer and the provider of some high-level structure/framework and the key imperatives for the discovery journey.<br><br>This requires a certain level of vulnerability-based trust from you as a leader. We'll look at this in more detail in Chapter VI: on T for TRUST. |

| Ingredients of enduring discomfort | How to build this leadership muscle |
|---|---|
| **Get out of your comfort zone.** | Don't be afraid of saying 'I don't know' and be a learner yourself.<br><br>Get comfortable working with people who are different from you in every way. In a 'mini me' culture, like-minded people limit or eliminate your competitiveness and originality. To get the most out of your team, you need cognitive diversity within your team, even if you feel uncomfortable working with very un-likeminded people with completely different behavioural styles. |
| **Manage negative emotions related to the discomfort,** for example, frustration, and worry. | If you fail to manage these negative emotions, you may end up with quick fixes and shortcuts that can derail you and your organisation from achieving your ultimate business goals.<br><br>Undercurrent negative emotions in teams can block the free flow of ideas and limit possibility thinking.<br><br>I once learnt an excellent technique to put aside negative emotions. I say to myself: Now I put the negative feeling, for example, worry, aside. I will come back to it and deal with it at six o'clock today. And then at six o'clock I come back to it and reflect on my negative feelings. Usually, when I start thinking about it, I am more distanced and better able to herd my negative emotions into a positive channel. If you are a leader who wakes up at night, you usually suppress, ignore, and neglect your negative feelings during the day. |

| Ingredients of enduring discomfort | How to build this leadership muscle |
|---|---|
| **Disrupt yourself before others do it!** | Your odds of success will be 6 times higher and your revenue opportunity 20 times greater when you pursue a disruptive course (Johnson, 2015).<br><br>Play to your distinctive strengths. People tend to overvalue what they are not and undervalue what they are. Start focusing more on your uniqueness. Name what you do uniquely well that others don't!<br><br>Where do you shine? What makes you feel strong?<br><br>Feelings of cultural and intellectual entitlement kill innovation and leadership. For example, when organisations become too big, they stop exploring smaller, riskier but perhaps more profitable markets because the resulting revenues, especially at the beginning, won't affect their bottom line enough. However, every big business started small. When they stop disrupting themselves, they stop learning.<br><br>How can you overstep your own shadow?<br><br>How much do you appreciate those around you who have very different views, opinions, and approaches? |

| Ingredients of enduring discomfort | How to build this leadership muscle |
|---|---|
| **Take the right risks to capitalise on the opportunities that exist out there.** | There are two kinds of risks to distinguish: competitive risk and market risk (Johnson, 2015). Competitive risk means assessing what opportunities your product has, and whether you can compete and win, so it is worth pursuing. Market risk is when you don't know whether there is a market there, although there is a need not yet being met, so it is worth looking into.<br><br>Brain science also supports market risk over competitive risk. When you compete, your sympathetic nervous system mobilises your body for a fight-or-flight response and releases cortisol. Your body likes cortisol initially, but after a while when its rush levels off, cognitive functioning deteriorates; judgement, memory, and even the immune system will all decline. However, taking market risk involves a much healthier mental state and this is when creativity and innovation kick in. The best way to take on market risk is just to play where no one else is playing. Where do you take on way too much competitive risk? How and where can you find and take on market risk?<br><br>How and where can you play where no one else is playing? |

| Ingredients of enduring discomfort | How to build this leadership muscle |
|---|---|
| **Embrace mistakes;** look at mistakes as opportunities. | This is easier said than done, because how can you embrace mistakes?<br><br>First, keep communicating that failure is not bad, that failure is part of the creative process. Also make sure to differentiate between what kind of failures you mean, because not all failures are appreciated.<br><br>Second, demonstrate how you learn from your own mistakes. Acknowledge that you've made a mistake, share it, and tell others what your key learning about yourself was. How did it impact the results, the team, the organisation as a whole and what would you do differently next time? |

## Ingredient #3 – Be persistent and disciplined

I am blessed with two beloved family members who are artistically talented. My husband is a talented painter, but he did not persistently pursue his talent, even though he loved and still loves painting. My 13-year-old daughter inherited her artistic talent from her father and both her grandmothers. She paints and draws incredibly well. We keep telling her to make the most of her talent and that she needs to practise it diligently and persistently. This requires discipline which, at her age right now, is quite challenging. Somehow dealing with creativity is pretty much the same as dealing with the talents of my husband and daughter; it is a seed that will only grow into a beautiful plant or a tree if we nurture it, diligently water it, day after day.

**Table 2.3: Ingredient #3 – Be persistent and disciplined**

| Ingredients of being persistent and disciplined | How to build this leadership muscle |
|---|---|
| **Steady and rigorous, sweaty hard work.** | When it comes to brainstorming, creativity may appear to be a light and easy task but real disruptive ideas that are viable business opportunities require hard work. You need the energy to do it. In the chapters, R is for RESILIENCE and A is for AGILITY, we'll explore more how you can build a sustainable human enterprise that can renew and create on an ongoing basis. |
| **Do your homework,** prepare diligently. | What sources do you check daily to stay current with various trends, technical innovations, and business initiatives in the global market? Develop a habit of reading and exploring (i.e., doing your homework) before sharing and involving others in any discussions. |
| **Dig deeper to get to the bottom of it.** | Drilling skills, attention to detail, and discipline are needed to turn ideas into business opportunities. This is where analytical people can be part of the creative process. Without them the idea is just a bubble, remaining at face value a balloon that is easy to pop. Analytical people can contribute in two ways:<br><br>Research the idea at hand in detail and present findings to the team.<br><br>Ask critical questions ('why' and 'what happens if...') to test the risk level of the idea.<br><br>Your role as a leader is to determine how to make the best of their strengths in the creative process. |

| Ingredients of being persistent and disciplined | How to build this leadership muscle |
|---|---|
| **Recognise that there are no quick fixes and no shortcuts, but maybe there are some low-hanging fruit.** | It is hard to differentiate between quick fixes and shortcuts, which most of the time do not take you to the land of innovation, and low-hanging fruit. This must be part of everyday business. Low-hanging fruit not only help you to keep up the momentum but also feed your stakeholders with small crumbs of success. While quick fixes and shortcuts have their place in daily operations, they can kill real creativity and innovation. |
| **Anticipate the future and prepare for a future where creativity is key.** | This is very much linked to doing your homework. When you do your homework as a leader you need to explore and anticipate the future. Most leaders find this a very intriguing part because it is like a strategy game. You should do it with the leadership team. Of course, you can do it in regular leadership meetings, but I recommend setting aside a separate time for a 'Future Organisation 2.1 Strategic Game' meeting/workshop. Let your imagination take off. Explore many avenues including best-case and worst-case scenarios and wild ideas. It is like an augmented reality game. |
| **You must believe it to see it through.** | At the core of all the things we've mentioned lies in you as a leader strongly believing that what you are pursuing is worth it, that it is the right thing to do, and that it serves the best interests of all parties. The most challenging part of this is when you receive a business imperative directive from headquarters and you need to internalise it and find a way to strongly connect to it. Only after you believe it with intensity will it have an impact on the organisation and its future. Ask yourself if you believe in what you are doing and pursuing 100%? Do you believe so much in yourself and your organisation that whatever comes you will tackle it? This is relevant for the big picture as well as for a single idea. We'll explore this further in Chapter VI: T is for TRUST. |

## CREATIVITY and continuous improvement

Many leaders interviewed said that creativity plays an important part in continuous improvement, i.e., doing things better day after day. It is a bottom-up approach that applies to everyone. If you're good at continuous improvement, you improve constantly but unfortunately, this improvement is based more on looking backwards. Revenue, profitability, market share, and customer satisfaction are past-focused; these indices cannot point the way to the future. To be able to close the gap between what is and what might be is to use not only continuous improvement but also discontinuous improvement now and then. The latter helps an organisation to stay relevant and be ahead of its market.

## CREATIVITY and innovation

### How to break out and move towards innovation

To break out from a continuous improvement way of thinking now and then, you have to deal with your mental blocks. These mental blocks are hardwired in your brain because of an evolutionary survival mechanism: play safe to survive. You cannot get rid of these blocks, but you can use techniques that help you go around them. As Hall (2017) taught me, discontinuous improvement is a big step change. It's about doing things differently, forgetting about the current reality and completely transforming it. This has to be driven top-down in the organisation.

### What kinds of ideas best serve discontinuous improvement?

Novel and useless ideas best serve discontinuous improvement. Unfortunately, we tend to use ideas that are useful so we can implement them straight away. But, according to Hall (2017), useful kills novel. If you want a truly creative solution that is future-focused, you should first brainstorm and find novel and useless ideas. These ideas could be outrageous, crazy, even sometimes illegal, and amoral. Then grab hold of the novelty and explore it. Understand it. And afterwards, find a useful and moral way of delivering it.

### Mental blocks to creativity and innovation

#### 1. Thinking processes

We are conditioned by our school systems in *second-stage thinking (vertical thinking)* using the left side of the brain. It is about problem-solving: taking information, processing it, and generating outcomes. Useful ideas based on our experience usually come out during second-stage thinking. It is very quick. If you want useful ideas and to continuously improve, use second-stage thinking.

*First-stage thinking (lateral thinking),* i.e., right-brain thinking, should be used for creativity. Novelty comes from this side of the brain. Exploring the problem with the less used part of the brain takes longer as it can, and does, make a lot of new connections between neurons, and therefore, it is very slow.

#### 2. Patterning systems

We break down information into patterns based on information from the past. They help us process a vast amount of information very quickly. It is great for problem-solving. Our brain has an

> enormous virtual filing cabinet full of patterns of everything and anything we have ever made sense of (Hall, 2017). If we get information that does not match data in our filing cabinet, the brain brushes it away and ignores it. Patterns of how we do things make us comfortable.
>
> When you have a pattern in your head you can't get rid of it. The disadvantage of these patterning systems is that they block your creativity. Various techniques can help you mess up your patterning systems and liberate your creativity.

When I profile leaders, I can recognise straight away those who find it challenging to get rid of or put aside their impressive filing cabinets. These leaders are very structured and systematic in their approach and highly analytical and accurate.

You can overcome these mental blocks by using various creativity techniques like Six Thinking Hats (Bono, 2017), Lego, and Superheroes (Idea Centre Group, 2022).

Why does creativity matter so much? Because it is the engine for innovation. It requires lots of energy, a vision, and trust in the unknown. It moves you forward, never backward. It is essential for crossing boundaries. It is an active process to bridge the gap between everyday work and sought-after innovation.

While creativity is about the generation of novel and useful ideas, innovation is about making money and adding value from creativity and the implementation of ideas.

Turning creativity into money is the real competitive advantage. As Steve Jobs (2018) said "Innovation is saying 'no' to 1000 things."

### Reflection points

- What kind of organisation do you want to build?
- What kind of future do you want to create and how are you going to do it?
- How can you introduce novelty into your organisation?
- How can you make your people think more out of the box, and generate novel and useful ideas?
- How can you create an environment in your organisation where there is a place and process for discontinuous improvement, creativity, and innovation?
- Which ingredients of the CREATIVITY cocktail are over- or under-represented in your leadership team? In your organisation? Cultivate curiosity? Endure discomfort? Be persistent and disciplined?

## CREATIVITY and strategy

"Earlier we had 5-year plans for companies. Today that plan is the equivalent of an exercise in creativity" (Morgan, 2020). Today's globalisation has generated a new demand for leaders. They need to expand their leadership capability of being able to not only create a vision but to create the future as well. I believe one of the keys to competitiveness is how much creativity and innovation potential an organisation has. I like working with leaders around the concept of the Blue Ocean Strategy and Blue Ocean Shift (Kim and Mauborgne, 2005; 2017) to turn on their creativity while strategizing. These books are a must-read for leaders as they discuss key messages related to unleashing the creative potential in you and your organisation.

"The only way to beat the competition is to stop trying to beat the competition" (Kim and Mauborgne; 2005, 2017). How powerful and inspiring is this? According to their theory, there are two types of oceans.

## Red Ocean vs Blue Ocean

Industries never stand still; they constantly evolve, especially in the fast digital advancement era. The overriding focus of strategic thinking has been competition-based; therefore, it is very much in line with Red Ocean strategies. But the results of such thinking are the accelerated commoditization of products and services, price wars, and shrinking profit margins. Before we get into how creativity has an important role in strategizing and especially moving more into Blue Ocean strategies, let's be clear about the difference between the Red Ocean and the Blue Ocean.

**Red Ocean** represents all the industries in existence today. It is a well-known market space, where industry boundaries are defined and accepted. The competitive rules of the game are known as companies try to outperform their rivals. The Red Ocean is getting increasingly crowded with the prospects for profit and growth limited and reduced. Products have become commodities with the cutthroat competition turning the Red Ocean bloody. There is only incremental improvement, with more number-crunching exercises and value-cost trade-offs (higher value delivered with higher cost). Red Oceans will always matter and will always be a fact of business life.

There is more place here for automatization, operational effectiveness, simplification, AI, and volume creation. But here, there is a limit.

Globalisation supports these dimensions and apart from the crowded market and fierce competition, we can see that the life span of companies is projected to shrink from 60 years to 14 years by 2026 (Morgan, 2020).

**Blue Ocean** industries are not yet in existence. It's about an unknown market space. There's demand creation in the untapped market and significant opportunity for highly profitable growth. The Blue Ocean is expanding existing industry boundaries. The rules of the game are waiting to be set. Value innovation is the cornerstone of Blue Ocean strategy, because it breaks the value-cost trade-off (you can deliver higher value with lower cost).

Expanding your horizon, seeing more and before (Maxwell, 2018) will give you the power to make a Blue Ocean strategic move. It does not need to be a completely new market or solution but something that creates a leap in value for customers, for the company, and for people. Cirque du Soleil is a great example of this.

Value innovation is creating a leap in value. In many cases, value creation is not enough; you also need value innovation by pursuing differentiation and low costs simultaneously. To achieve that, you will need to visit your industry and redefine the problem the industry focuses on, by asking the following questions:

| Eliminate | Raise |
|---|---|
| Which factors that the industry has long competed on should be eliminated? | Which factors should be raised well above the industry's standard? |
| **Reduce** | **Create** |
| Which factors should be reduced well below the industry's standard? | Which factors should be created that the industry has never offered? |

**Figure 2.2: The ERRC grid (Kim and Mauborgne, 2017).**

When you try to answer these questions, you should consider not only competitors but also shift to alternative industries or from customers to non-customers.

### Reflection points

- Where is your business reality?
- In which direction are you sailing your craft?
- How many crafts of your fleet are sailing on the Red Ocean and how many on the Blue Ocean?
- How bloody is your Red Ocean?
- What are the weather conditions?
- How could you focus more on the Blue Ocean instead of the Red Ocean?
- How do you steer your craft?
- What kind of craft do you have?

According to Kim and Mauborgne (2005; 2017), leaders often accept and wrongly act on two fundamental assumptions:

1. Market boundaries and industry conditions are given. You cannot change them; you have to build your strategy based on them.
2. To succeed within these environmental constraints, an organisation must make a strategic choice between differentiation and low cost.

I have heard quite a few self-limiting and 'glass-half-full' types of responses from leaders based on these assumptions. However, to break out from the bloody competition, both assumptions have to be taken down. When done, there is a huge opportunity to bring creativity to life and create something more valuable than before.

Leaders spend most of their strategic thinking time on filling in boxes and running numbers instead of getting a clear picture of how to break from the competition with creative strategizing.

Even if you feel that your circle of influence is limited, you need to learn and step up your game; otherwise, you will not be impactful. You may end up letting your people down as a result. You need to learn how to reconstruct the given market conditions to create the future.

Kim and Mauborgne (2005; 2017) show how to reconstruct market boundaries by exploring possibilities using the 6 paths framework:

1. Look across alternative industries' offerings.
2. Look across strategic groups within industries.
3. Look across the chain of buyers.
4. Look across complementary products and services.
5. Look across functional or emotional offerings that appeal to buyers.
6. Look across time.

When you are turning your spotlight onto these 6 paths, many questions can be asked. What can you see there? What opportunities do they hold? What are the advantages/disadvantages of those opportunities? What are your buyers' pain points? What are the biggest costs the current offering imposes on buyers? How can you recognise currently unconnected dots, fragments worth pursuing for future creation? Over the horizon what trends will impact your industry?

## Pursuing a market-creating strategy with a leadership mindset shift

The business market is facing increasingly intense competition and margin pressure. In this market, leaders often accept and act on the two fundamental assumptions we discussed earlier. Growth can be achieved from two directions (Kim and Mauborgne, 2005; 2017):

- **Disruptive creation** captures the full, not partial, opportunity space of market creation driven by displacement. For example, cassettes were replaced by CDs, and then CDs were replaced by MP3s.
- **Non-disruptive creation** creates new market space without disrupting an existing market. For example, many men's lives were revolutionised through Pfizer's market-creating move of Viagra.

There are 3 ways of pursuing a market-creating strategy according to Blue Ocean Strategy (Kim and Mauborgne, 2005; 2017):

1. **Offer a breakthrough solution for an existing industry problem.**

Breakthrough solutions create new demands and convert non-customers into customers. Just think how many more people take photos today with digital cameras than they did with cameras with film in the past.

2. **Redefine and solve an existing industry problem.**

Problem redefinitions allow any organisation to replace assumptions and reconstruct industry boundaries in new and creative ways. Here, both disruptive and non-disruptive creation is in full play. The most famous example is Cirque du Soleil. They redefined their problem of cheap services in a rapidly declining industry by focusing on how to maximise the fun and thrill of the circus, how to combine the best of it – clowns, tents, and amazing acrobats – with the best of theatre and ballet – their artistry, music, dance, and storylines. They eliminated costly and controversial elements like animals creating a new market space between these industries, pulling in new people, for example, adults without children and corporate clients who had never dreamed of going to a circus before.

3. **Identify and solve a brand-new problem or seize a brand-new opportunity.**

Unlock new markets beyond existing industry boundaries. Sesame Street's Muppets (Big Bird, Elmo, Ernie, and Bert) teach preschool children to count, name colours, and recognise shapes and the letters of the alphabet in such a fun way that they hardly realise they are learning. Sesame Street did not disrupt any prior market for childhood education. Rather it opened up a new value-cost frontier that unlocked a new market of preschool edutainment that had never existed before.

## What kind of mindset do you need as a leader for this creative strategizing?

- Make the competition irrelevant; step away from the benchmarks.
- Focus on creating and capturing new demands. Listen to potential buyers and non-buyers. Look at Steve Jobs. No one wanted an iPhone but he created the demand and made sure people would.
- Invite different perspectives to the table for discussion.
- Set out to reshape industry conditions as we live in an era when disruption is a must.

- Expand your field of vision.
- Shift your thinking from constraints to new opportunities.
- Ask fundamentally different sets of questions (this book will help you there).
- Simultaneously pursue differentiation and low cost.

Making this shift can be achieved with creativity and innovation by any organisation, be it for-profit, non-profit, public, a big multinational company, or a small enterprise.

### Reflection points

- Create a list of key factors your industry currently competes on.
- Which of the factors that the industry takes for granted should be eliminated?
- Which factors should be reduced well below the industry's standard?
- Which factors should be raised well above the industry's standard?
- Which factors that the industry has never offered should be created?

As you can see, creativity has a place not only in everyday business, but in continuous improvement, innovation, and strategizing. Now, let's move to where you become a CREATOR by tuning into your leadership craft.

## The leader as a CREATOR

Leaders play a significant role in creation. As Peter Drucker put it "The best way to predict the future is to create it" (cited in Williamson, 1986:149).

### What exactly do you as a leader need to CREATE?

- Place and time for creativity for your and for your people.
- The environment and conditions for creativity and innovation. (e.g., rituals, platforms, creative rooms; 10% of the time can be allocated to generate new business ideas).
- A leap in value for your people, the clients, and the organisation. This is an ongoing exercise for you and the organisation.
- Clarity for direction, and craft strategic conversations within your organisation to reinforce key imperatives and obtain buy-in.
- Platforms for co-creation. Creativity is not a one-(wo)man-show; it never was and never will be.
- A new uncontested market space that makes the competition irrelevant. Don't undervalue your real and potential role in it, no matter where you are coming from as a leader (country head of a multinational company or CEO-owner of a local SME).
- Alignment through leadership communication. Communicate with mind and heart and with frequency. Develop stories and metaphors to communicate. Develop channels to reinforce your message. What is the most important message you want to convey to your people about creativity and innovation?

After reading this list, write 2 or 3 specific examples of what and how you will do that in your day-to-day leadership operation.

Nothing mentioned in this chapter can be achieved without doing all your homework as a leader. You should never outsource your eyes, ears, mouth, or most importantly your heart. Do your own homework!

## CRAFTING the future

Finally, the ultimate goal to master the leadership quality for CREATIVITY and CREATE is CRAFTING the future. When you CRAFT the future, you create a market. You create jobs. You create the future for yourself and others.

Unfortunately, adaptability is essential, but not sufficient today. If you are adapting to the market changes you are following, you are already behind. This is why you need to create the future.

Every business is a people's business. You must give people a reason to believe and join you and your company. They need a reason to commit. Whatever you CRAFT, it must have a greater impact on society because today everything is interconnected. You need to broaden the scope of your leadership responsibility. This requires the courage to step up; it cannot be achieved without mastering all 5 leadership qualities in CRAFT Leadership starting with C is for CREATIVITY and CREATE.

---

### Leadership insights

"Prior to the Covid-19 pandemic, the company's financial results were based on 10% local guests and 90% tourists from abroad. We had to look into how we could introduce additional services on top of the basic services, and move more towards national guests, to get the balance right. I had to do a lot of homework, look at what was happening in the world, and creatively adapt the ideas I learnt to our market, to our situation, to our current conditions. We had to see what the quick wins in this were and what we needed to build on in the long run. My role in that as a leader was to drive it all. I read a lot. I attended online conferences. I participated in the online events of the International SPA Association and shared my findings with the management team. Networking can play a big part in being inspired by others and hearing creative ideas outside of your own bubble. The next steps were to implement some of the ideas, for example, balneology, post-Covid treatments, the medical effects of the thermal water especially on stress derived from the pandemics, etc."

"How can you get the mammoth to innovate? One of the ways multinational organisations innovate is by the acquisition of innovative start-ups or small enterprises. When a huge multinational conglomerate, a big monster, acquires a start-up, the challenge is that the culture of the flexible start-up seems to be alien to the culture of the big organisation. The immune system of the big organisation rejects it. One solution is to run the start-up on the periphery, to give people time to get used to each other. The newcomers start educating the big organisation. Workshops dismantle traditional panels and rigid thinking mechanisms, and educate the big organisation about the new methods and mindsets."

"The greatest challenge recently was to fill our 'old school' Research and Development (R&D) Division with very smart PhD people in white coats, although they had zero connection to the buyers or to the market and very little to the sales division. In fact, they did not speak the same language. When the head of this 'old school' R&D left, we had to rethink how to turn this division into a market-oriented innovative one. We had to decide who would be the next leader and how to build a more diverse team of people where many professions could be represented because maybe our next new solution wouldn't be medicine but a piece of software. To face the truth, we had to change something that was the soul of the company before and turn it into something modern. It was hard in itself but selling it to the leadership team and the organisation was even harder. However, we had to do it. We had to create an R&D Division which was able to stay relevant and address the very complex issues of our industry and our market innovatively."

---

Are you ready to move to the next quality in order to CRAFT the future for yourself and others?

# CHAPTER III

## R is for RESILIENCE

"A good half of the art of living is resilience."

(Alain de Botton, cited in Eggers and Barlow, 2019:41)

### The definition and importance of RESILIENCE

Resilience is an essential modern leadership quality if you are to thrive and survive. It's the 'R' from the CRAFT Leadership model.

The definition of resilience I heard from Dr Rose Aghdami during one of her workshops goes like this: "The ability to recognise, face and adapt well to stress and adversity. The best safeguard against anxiety, stress and burnout." Resilience means partly being resistant, or having the ability to bounce back, and partly flexible, or having the ability to adapt to new circumstances, new conditions.

"Resilience relates to the ability to respond well to adversity, which could apply to a wide range of challenging events, from the trivial and annoying to the truly tragic. Resilient people demonstrate emotional intelligence and exhibit a high level of self and social awareness along with an ability to effectively manage themselves and their relationship with others, especially under strain" (Jawad–Kakabadse 2019: 113).

I define resilience as the ability to recognise when you need to stand like a rock, and when you need to swim with the current and act with confidence and ease.

Resilience is the capability of individuals to understand and creatively draw on their internal and external strengths, resulting in effective coping with challenges and significant adversity in ways that promote health, wellness, and an increased ability to respond constructively to future adversity (Hammond, 2008, in Simpson-Yuen, 2018).

Resilience is the ability to survive a setback (a singular event) and adversity (a continuous experience). It is bending and not breaking, not only surviving but thriving in adversity and crises. One leader I spoke to had this to say:

> "How to appreciate heaven, when you have never been to hell? Sometimes we need to experience hard hits to know what is really important and what to go back to. Things may seem completely hopeless, but everything is relative and subjective. It depends on the basis of all comparisons; it is part of the learning, learning to be resilient up and down in the whole organisation."

Resilience has flexibility at its core. As a resilient person, you can face difficult experiences in life and work with flexible thoughts, feelings, and behaviours. Resilience is not just seeing and dealing with difficulties. An important part of resilience is having the confidence to face situations that could be challenging and difficult, believing that whatever comes your way, you will be able to manage and reach a positive outcome in time. The good news is that resilience is not inborn; it can be learnt. We all have some resilience, and whatever we have can be further developed.

## What happens when you are being disrupted by stressors?

According to Hans Selye's General Adaptation Syndrome theory (Selye, 1951), there is a stressor and there are 3 phases based on how long this stressor affects you and how much you can resist it (Figure 3.1).

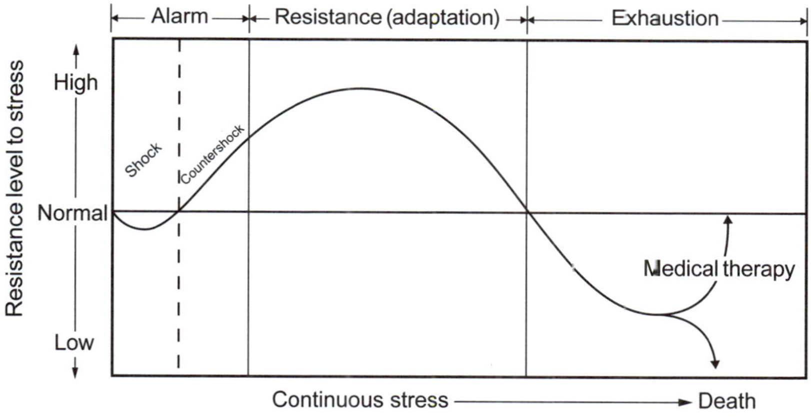


**Figure 3.1: General Adaptation Syndrome (Brown and Waslien, 2003).**

- **Alarm reaction:** An instinctive reaction – fight or flight response – kicks in. The sympathetic nervous system is activated. Hormones such as adrenaline and cortisol are released into your bloodstream to meet the danger or threat. In everyday life as a leader, you'll need to learn how to push your invisible internal pause button to give yourself time to breathe and not to get emotionally hijacked. This will give you time to develop an intentional response to these impulses and stressors.

- **Active resistance/adaptation:** Your body is still on alert. The adrenaline and cortisol levels are still high, but your body starts both collecting resources and trying to meet the stressor. If the resistance stage continues for too long of a period without pauses to counterbalance the effects of stress, this can lead to the exhaustion stage. Signs of the resistance stage include irritability, frustration, and poor concentration.
- **Burn out or exhaustion phase:** If the stressor continues to affect your body, sooner or later it will become fatigued and then burn out.

What does it mean? The adaptation energy of the body is limited and exhaustible. After the initial alarm reaction, your body either adapts or resists. But burnout or fatigue will occur eventually, if you don't deal with it.

## Anecdote 3. "I will never burn out..."

A couple of years ago, I had a developmental conversation on the topic of renewal and energy management with a regional leader who was responsible for 14 counties. He had been in a top leadership role for more than 14 years. He had a family with 4 children. He told me that he travelled a lot. Every week he was on the road visiting offices and key clients at least in 4 countries. When I asked him about the risk of burning out, he said "Look Beáta, I love what I do and I think if someone loves what he does, he will never get burnt out." He considered the conversation closed and was ready to move on. I asked him another question: "Do you agree that we human beings have physical limitations?" He said he did. I went on:

"Do you agree that not only things but we ourselves can be worn out?" He agreed. "Because," I continued, "if we don't take care of ourselves, we can be worn out, and we can easily get broken." I led the conversation in this direction because I have experienced a complete breakdown. I held 3 positions (local, regional, and global) at the same time, something I enjoyed immensely. I asked again: "What mechanisms do you have in place to prevent yourself from being burnt out? How do you take care of yourself? When do you know that you've pushed yourself too far? When it is too late?" That was the point when the conversation moved onto another level, addressing not only the here and now of his leadership but also his sustainable leadership modus operandi for the future.

## Anecdote 4. Take care of your key talents

Another experience that made me include RESILIENCE in the 5 CRAFT Leadership qualities was how leadership candidates in one organisation were and are being treated and sadly let down by their leaders. These key talents were very passionate and eager to jump into challenging, complex new assignments. They were high performers with high potential. As they were motivated, hard workers with lots of energy, they were booked on the biggest assignments all the time, so the organisation constantly put pressure on them. The talents didn't pay attention to their energy budgets, and they also didn't dare to and couldn't say no to leaders, partly because their inner drivers wouldn't allow them to be left out, and partly because they wanted to meet and exceed expectations. As a result, most of them burnt out or reached their limit of almost burning out. When they were appointed leaders, top leadership was surprised to see that these newly appointed leaders had lost their passion and their drive. I saw one of these burnt-out key talents fall apart and when it happened, she was labelled as mentally unstable. I was angry. It was as much the fault of the organisation as of the individual. It is the responsibility of HR and the leadership team to look after their talents and not to exploit them. Building their muscles in RESILIENCE is key here.

Our adaptation capabilities are limitless, but our adaptation energy is not. However, our world is full of disruptions, some of them good, some of them not so good; nevertheless, its constant flow puts enormous pressure on leaders.

### Reflection points

- What is your approach to the unexpected? How do you respond to stress? How do you manage the inner and outer turbulence of today's world?
- Can you survive setbacks? Can you work through adversity?
- As a leader, how do you prevent yourself from getting fatigued or burnt out?
- Do you have an energy budget?
- Where do you lose/gain energy during work?
- What does resilience mean for you as a leader?
- As a leader, when do you need to stand like a rock and when do you need to swim with the current?

In this chapter, we explore what a resilient leader and a resilient organisation look like according to the leaders I interviewed. What are the threats to resilience? And we look into the 5 key elements of becoming a resilient leader:

- Flexibility in thinking to enhance RESILIENCE
- Flexibility in feeling to embrace your inner RESILIENCE
- Resourcefulness as the road to RESILIENCE
- Anchors as the rocks underneath RESILIENCE
- Skilful energy management in mastering RESILIENCE

## The resilient leader

Most of the leaders I interviewed agreed that there is no resilient organisation without a resilient leader and resilient people in it.

When you become more resilient, you are better equipped to build an organisation that is resilient enough to innovate, sustain, and come back strong in environments of rapid and disruptive change. Resilience is required for navigation through the VUCA world in which you live.

It is important to note that resilience cannot be built in times of crisis. You must build resilience intentionally before it is even needed. It is not only about survival but also about learning how to thrive under pressure and difficult conditions, to emerge almost transformed by the experience, coming out stronger afterwards.

Today, resilience is not only about bouncing back but it also is about bouncing forward so that you emerge stronger from a stressful situation and crisis. It is about moving forward more energised, elevated, and equipped for what is next. Some may say that there is no such thing as bouncing back anymore due to the many disruptions we face today, but there are fundamentals that can be considered as the rocks that give you and your organisation the stability you need.

Resilient leaders...

- do not bounce back all the time as they might have in the past. Bouncing back is only a part of resilience, and in today's environment, it has become a smaller, albeit important, part of it.
- are not immune to adversity; they don't have the skin of a rhinoceros.
- are not naively positive, only seeing the positive side of things, not facing facts and reality. It is essential that a leader not only navigates their craft into the targeted harbours but prepares their people and their organisation for future adversities and storms.
- are not cold, detached, and distant towards others and in relation to issues. Not showing emotions, not showing vulnerability stops leaders from connecting to their people at the heart level, which is important for high employee engagement.
- don't constantly change and adapt and as a result, lose stability, lose their personal and organisational anchors, and their trust in the eyes of their people.

## Then what does a resilient leader look like?

- **Persistent:** "Keep rotating until you fit into" as one of the leaders said. Maintain focus and carry on delivering results while the environment around you explodes. It's about not throwing in the towel at the first hurdle or the fiftieth.
- **Resistant:** "Be the bastion of your organisation; this is what is expected of me," another leader reflected. Be the stable force, the rock for your people, especially at the level of values. Don't let your personal and organisational values trade off at any cost. This provides stability and a safety net for your people.

- **High level of endurance:** Some leaders said that one of the best attributes of a good leader is their ability to endure failure, to not get discouraged or overwhelmed by the number and complexity of the challenges they face. In leadership, there is no place for blame or saying, 'the problem is...' and pointing a finger. Owning the problems and learning from them is key here.
- **Shock-proof:** You should have a solid secondary survival mechanism in place, to be shock-proof, and resistant to being broken. It is like training your muscles, learning your limits, and having a support system in place. We, including you, all have our primary survival mechanism (the fight-flight-freeze response) but other than that you need to be able to handle the unexpected. Recovery sessions, when you or your organisation has been through a difficult time, help you become shock-proof, building an inner calmness or an external appearance of calmness.
- **Uncertainty tolerant:** The most challenging part of dealing with a crisis is maintaining a high level of self-motivation and not losing sight of your vision and perspective. You need to have an internal engine of resourcefulness and drive to motivate yourself and your organisation. Also, you should have a mechanism to vent accumulated, unnecessary frustration.
- **Flexible:** Be able to respond to changes in your environment both internally and externally with variety and speed.
- **Opportunistically optimistic:** Think in terms of opportunities. Even if you face negative events and their consequences, your role as a leader is to see that even these negative events may carry future opportunities. Think ahead and bear the pain now with a strong belief that it will turn out well because you did

your job of looking at the facts and preparing yourself and your organisation to face and handle these facts.

- **Manage your own emotions:** Be aware of your emotional responses and channel those emotions for the better.
- **Trustworthy:** Create a trusting environment. The stress level of the organisation very much depends on how much people trust their leadership and whether you can create a circle of safety for your people. People who feel the trusted support of their leader are more resilient.
- **Adopt the 'one for all and all for one' approach:** Know that the team as a whole is much more resilient than any one person. But when creativity kicks in, things and people can run in hundreds of directions. Your role as a leader is to keep them on track. Being focused is essential (3 of the CRAFT qualities have just been mentioned here: CREATIVITY-RESILIENCE-FOCUS). The organisation reflects the image of the leader.
- **See and show the why:** Never lose sight of the meaning, the why. This is where your heart is and the heart of your people. When your heart is involved, you and your organisation can bear a lot and move mountains.
- **Practise and role-model self-care:** Build and stretch muscles in physical, emotional, mental, and spiritual fitness. This includes not only high-intensity training in all dimensions but recovery periods as well.
- **Seek out social and professional support:** A resilient leader is not afraid of reaching out for help when needed. Make sure that you create space for social interaction, family gatherings, and meeting friends regularly. We are, after all, social animals.

## Leadership insights

"To endure and survive when the market crashes is resilience but this is not enough. How you can not only maintain your business in difficult market conditions but be able to find new opportunities, new ways of delivering value to customers, or find and start operating in a brand-new market to prosper, now that is resilience for me."

"I have never been non-resilient. I have a strong survival instinct. Resilience has a lot of levels. For me, it is more like being shockproof, which should be handled in a much broader sense. It is the ability to deal with stressful situations cool-headedly by consciously creating space for the emotional part. Nevertheless, for me it is more expedient sometimes to set the emotions aside and to be able to deal with the task at hand, to see what lesson we can learn by going forward, which is not always positive. However, at the end of the day, I must come back to deal with the emotional stuff. The family, my partner, and sports play important parts in it. I consciously shut down as well as shut out people who drain my energy. I consciously check what is important in it, or I put it on a separate track and run it down there. If I can find key learning points, I put the whole matter at a resting point fast. If I cannot, now that is particularly stressful for me."

"The resilient leader does not panic; they cannot be shocked in any situation. They are characterised by calmness and composure, keep the given situation in proper balance, have a high level of self-control, and can keep the team in focus."

"Now I don't feel resilient. I just always push the bounce forward. I constantly force it. I force the organisation to adapt all the time, but you know what, you can burn the organisation out if you don't make plateaus in it. So, this is a red flag for me."

## The resilient organisation

As I mentioned before, there is no resilient organisation without a resilient leader and resilient people in it. An organisation mirrors its leaders. Let's see what leaders said about resilient organisations.

> "The challenge here is to make the organisation permanently resilient, provided that there is such a thing as permanent resilience. Because without running out of energy we constantly need to find new solutions to current and future problems and situations."

A resilient organisation is one where there is always someone who bites and someone who rests. The resilient organisation is sustainable, and focused on the long term. At the same time, it is always being renewed during change. These organisations have internal reserves; they can tap into their hidden resources and operate more effectively and efficiently.

> "You have reserves if you work along a good strategy. If you don't have a good strategy every day is a struggle."

They also highlighted the importance of alignment and re-alignment of the organisation. To achieve that, they have to push the pause button from time to time to check and get clear on whether they are still on the right track before they act. In resilient organisations, people can connect to a meaningful future vision. They are empowered to work towards that vision. Resilient companies set out to find a Blue Ocean niche to develop unique capabilities so there will be no competitors. There is no need for them to compromise their values and be pushed into a fee/price competition. The change-able and change-capable organisation is resilient and knows where and how to be flexible.

## Threats to RESILIENCE and strategies to cope

There are two main threats to resilience: stress and burnout in leadership.

### Leadership stress and burnout

Stress is one of the main plagues of modern times. Of course, there is 'good' stress and 'bad' stress. Some stress can help improve your mental and physical performance and some can drain you. You can recognise this when you perform much better under stress or time pressure.

The 'bad' stress could be when you are facing pressure over a long period, say from shareholders, employees, and the firm's largest customers. According to Dr Rose Aghdami (2018), there are many causes of stress at work: perceived or actual overwork, perceived or actual lack of control, difficult relationships, loss of confidence, and toxic pressure.

The danger of this could be either burning out at an earlier stage or suddenly dropping dead of a heart attack before hitting 50. What is happening? You live and operate in a turbulent, fast-paced world, which lessens your internal and external sense of control.

Due to technological advancement and data overflow, you have more emails in your inbox than you can handle daily. You may work long hours and attend functions and dinners outside working hours. Your days are jammed with back-to-back meetings, sometimes with triple clashes. Sales targets and profitability reports and presentations vie for attention. Today's business environment is obsessively goal-oriented with moving targets, which makes you forget about celebrating the successes. But isn't that all part of being in an executive/leadership role?

Can you recognise any of the following signs?

- Constantly worrying about work.
- Feeling overwhelmed and unable to cope.
- Always feeling rushed and pressured.
- Feeling stuck in one place.
- Bringing the stress of work home to your family and friends.
- Having difficulty falling or staying asleep.
- Constantly feeling angry/frustrated with yourself or others.
- Finding it difficult to make quick and timely decisions because of how they will impact your business.
- Thinking that you are the only one feeling this way within the leadership team; therefore, you just need to try harder and conceal it, mask it.
- Constantly being on your phone, tablet, or laptop – even while driving or eating – or on your days off.
- Having headaches, back pain, aching joints, and abdominal tightness.
- Drinking more alcohol, smoking more cigarettes, taking more recreational/prescription drugs, gambling more to make you 'feel better'.

Remember that stressors can be opportunities too, depending on your filters. We will have a look at how to change or reframe your filters later in this chapter.

To have a strong grip and sharpen your leadership presence there are many excellent mindfulness exercises you could do regularly or whenever you feel the need. Let's explore two:

### 1) Emptying your mind exercise

Close your eyes or fix them on a spot. Imagine a gently flowing stream with leaves floating on the surface of the water. For the next 2 minutes take every thought that pops into your head, whether it's a picture or a word, and place it on top of a leaf and let it float by. Do this for every thought, whether it's positive or negative, happy or sad, and see what happens. The aim is to step back from your thoughts and just watch their natural flow. If you're thinking: 'This is silly' or 'This is too hard' or 'I can't do it', or 'I'm not sure if I'm doing this right' put those thoughts on leaves too. You don't have to challenge your thoughts or squash them. Just let them come and go as if they were boats sailing by. If uncomfortable feelings show up like impatience, anxiety, or frustration, say silently to yourself: 'noticing frustration' or 'noticing anxiety' and place those words onto a leaf and let it float down the stream. From time to time you'll get hooked and your mind will go off in a different direction, for example to the things on your to-do list, what you need to buy for dinner, what date your report is due. Simply acknowledge this and start the exercise again from the beginning. This will help you to empty your mind and heart in the middle of the day between two meetings.

## 2) Let go/let in/let be – a mindfulness exercise

**The principle of this exercise:**

**Let go** – Letting go of anything that may get in the way, anything that is disturbing you, or anything that keeps you in the past or stuck.

**Let in** – Creating space for new things or for unknown things that may not have surfaced yet.

**Let be** – Experiencing and embracing the 'here and now' by observing and noticing things around you, enjoying the moment on the journey, and learning from the experience as it goes.

Begin with sitting in a comfortable posture with your back straight and your feet on the floor. You can either close your eyes or allow your gaze to dissolve into a soft diffused vision in front of you. Bring your attention to your breathing. Take a deep breath a couple of times then start paying attention to your regular breathing, in and out, in and out.

**Let go:** When you breathe out you let go of whatever holds you tight, and anything that disturbs your mind. Keep repeating, breathing out the tension, the confrontation you just had, the barriers you see, and so on. You can either do this exercise only or combine it with the others.

**Let in:** Now, when you feel you have emptied the tension from your mind and let go of whatever is stuck there, turn your focus to your breathing again. Breathe in and breathe out, in and out, in and out. This time while repeating the breathing in and out, watch what might emerge through the exercise when you breathe in. If it is something connected to the disturbing part, again breathe out, let it go.

**Let be:** The third element of this exercise is purely focusing on breathing (in and out, in and out) and noticing your body, your breathing, and your surroundings without any judgement, comment, or thought. It will sharpen your senses and bring you more into the here and now.

You can do these exercises for 2–10 minutes as you wish, separately or all together.

## Stress coping mechanism

You need to turn the volume up on your stress coping mechanism today, especially in times of adversity and crisis. Again, what works well differs for everyone. Daily exercise is essential for various reasons. For example, if you are quarantined for any reason, you need to exercise regularly. If you don't, you won't get physically tired and that will impact your sleeping habits and your mood as well.

Easy stress-release mechanisms to implement:

**Cardio** is the best way to channel out your negative energy and stress. It also generates positive hormones that help you see things more positively.

**Laughter** is a great way to release stress, for example when you watch comedies.

**News control:** Don't watch/read news updates 24/7, especially during a crisis. Although it is important to be well informed as a leader, you should try to restrict yourself to watching the news twice a day as it has an enormous impact on your productivity, your energy management, and your mood.

### Strategies to de-stress in the moment

**When you have one minute**

- Take a few deep breaths and think "I am" as you breathe in and "calm" as you breathe out.
- Stretch your body and roll your shoulders.
- Take regular daily breaks from technology and just walk around, saying positive kind words to your people or asking them how they are.
- Drink lots of water.

**When you have 10 minutes**

- Take time out in your mind – visualise yourself relaxing in your peaceful place. Meditate.
- Go for a brisk walk. A 10-minute walk can improve your mood for around two hours.

Choose 2 techniques/actions and start using them daily to further develop your resilience and beat stress and burnout.

Let's move on and explore further how to build your resilience muscles as a leader. You must develop yourself in these 5 areas:

## Flexibility in thinking to enhance RESILIENCE

To become more resilient, increase your flexibility in thinking by looking at how you think on your feet, how you reflect on your feet, how you unleash your endless potential of possibility thinking, and how you turn up the volume on your creative thinking.

## Thinking on your feet

It's important to optimise your brain fitness so that you not only understand and see through complex problems swiftly but you are also able to learn, unlearn, and relearn in a limited time, which helps you think quickly and sharply on your feet at any given situation. I will explore this in more detail at Neuro-Agility in Chapter IV: A is for AGILITY.

## Reflecting on your feet

Realise that the desired result can no longer be achieved with the same solution model, in the same way, with the same thinking. And at the heart of this recognition is constant reflection. Reflect on what is working and what is not working. Constantly evaluate yourself and the organisation against whatever benchmark(s) you use.

## Unleashing the potential of possibility thinking

One of the most important survival and thriving techniques is reframing. You as a leader need to do it a lot, not only for yourself but for the whole organisation. When facing many challenges, problems, and difficulties, ask yourself what the opportunity in this is, what the tiniest potential in this, what learning you can take out of this, what tiny steps you can take to move forward even if you don't know what forward means yet. You cannot achieve this without valuing ideas and exploring all the known and unknown options.

### Turning up the volume on creative thinking

In Chapter II: C is for CREATIVITY and CREATE, we saw how creativity and creating play an important role in modern leadership. Nevertheless, to enhance resilience you need to be more flexible in your thinking as a leader. Turning up the volume on your creative thinking is essential. Be the champion of thinking out of the box. Continually challenge the status quo by asking questions starting with 'why' or 'why not. Connect dots that have never been imagined as connected. Create an environment where creative thinking has its place with built-in rituals. This is paramount in your role as a leader.

Creativity blooms when there is a culture of failure within the organisation, whereby you let your people experiment without fear of failure. Because of these experiments, new creative ideas emerge. It is counter-intuitive to embrace failure as failure is very much connected to negative feelings. Why should you embrace anything that makes you feel bad? The greatest oxymoron of today's advancement is to celebrate failure. It is not only a mind-tangling game but also an emotional one.

## Flexibility in feeling to embrace your inner RESILIENCE

Flexibility in feeling comes from different sources. Be aware of your range of feelings. Know you can feel in control without overcontrolling anything or anyone. Learn how to cope with negative emotions in order not to let them interfere or hijack you. Have compassion for yourself and for others, which can be very challenging in the hyper-achieving culture of an organisation.

## Being aware of a range of feelings

When crisis and adversity hit, you are less driven by your rational brain as the emotional part of you is being hijacked by the turmoil of the crisis. A lot is happening at the emotional level. The amygdala, the emotional brain, shuts down your rational thinking under stress. Therefore, you have to bring your FOCUS down to the smallest elements and keep it there at a transactional level. But emotions shouldn't be left there unattended; they should be picked up later on either with support or as part of your leadership reflection routine. But parking your emotions even for a short period can help you be resilient as a leader in a difficult situation.

## Feeling in control

We have a natural tendency to fight to maintain control, no matter whether it is real control or perceived control. According to studies (Aghdami, 2018), stress is not caused by the higher degree of responsibility and pressure usually associated with rank. It is not the demands of the job that cause the most stress, but the degree of control people feel they have throughout their day. Simply said: less control, more stress.

If you are trying furiously to control situations to feel less stressed, you are actually not in control at all. Having a strong internal sense of power and control is essential to managing your thoughts, and more importantly your feelings and emotions, and keeping your stress and anxiety levels well under control.

Short-term pay-offs can bring you relief. Beware of wanting to feel control in the moment in the form of micro management as you might pay a price in the long term, such as lower trust, disengagement, and a lack of innovation and collaboration. Aim for or be willing to pay the shorter-term price for a longer-term payoff. Coaching is a classic example. Coaching someone takes longer than giving precise instructions. But they will not learn how to think for themselves if they're simply told what to do as it creates a lack of ownership and proactiveness.

## Coping with negative emotions

To cope with negative emotions and become more resilient, be clear about two things. The first is that your thoughts are your reality. The second is that feelings follow thoughts and behaviours follow feelings. This is what is called a vicious or virtuous cycle.

Learn to reign your thoughts and develop a more realistic, positive mindset, which is also explored in Chapter IV: A is for AGILITY. Let's look at how you can control your negative emotions with your thinking. First of all, challenge the unhelpful 'What if?' thinking by asking yourself the following questions:

- Is there any evidence to support my views?
- Is there any evidence against my views?
- Are my thoughts rational?
- Am I catastrophizing?
- What would I advise someone in a similar situation?
- What is the worst-case scenario?

Although this is a thinking process, it helps quickly turn negative emotions into positive ones. Learning how to do this can help you embrace and unblock your inner resilience.

### Having compassion for self and others

Exercising compassion is important in adversity. Celebrating and learning from failure cannot be achieved without compassion. It is hard, as a leader, to have compassion for yourself, to role model overcoming struggles, and to have the courage to show vulnerability. Helping others is not only a selfless, kind act but it is also a bit selfish as it makes you feel good. Be compassionate, help others and you will feel better. You'll create a positive vibe and energy at a systemic level.

## Being resourceful is the road to RESILIENCE

The journey is less bumpy if you set off with ammunition, such as resources, choices, and strengths, and different scenarios and plans. There are various sources from which you can be refuelled: internal and external resources that you as a leader have and your organisation has, choices you can make, and your strengths and those of your organisation.

### Resources, choices, and strengths

When you have a long list of internal and external resources, choices, and individual and team strengths at your disposal, you and your organisation are more resilient. But to be, think, and feel it, you constantly need to take stock and show your people how resourceful you are. There is always more you can think of. You will be most effective when you can fully lean on the resources of other people in your life. If you fall, and you know that the other person will catch you, you will have more courage to walk into the unknown. Therefore, apart from taking stock of all the resources and sustainable future-forward inventory, as a leader you should intentionally design partnerships and alliances both internally and externally, to further tap into greater resources.

### Scenarios and plans

When there is adversity, your focus narrows to be able to survive. This is normal. However, as a leader, you have a role to provide a perspective for your people. And providing a perspective even in crisis is important because people get even more panicked if they feel they have no perspective, no future, no hope. How can you do that when you don't know how far this crisis will escalate? Scenario planning is one of the tools you can use. Create scenarios, 'what if' plans. Create plan B, plan C, plan D, etc., for yourself and your organisation. You will realise you have more options, more choices at hand than you thought. You also will be more prepared; it helps you control not the situation but the chaos.

When you are burnt out, stressed, or overworked you have limited access to your own resources. If you are resourceful, you are more resilient and respond more effectively to adversity.

## Anchors as the rocks underneath RESILIENCE

Here is one of the fundamental questions related to resilience. When do you stand like a rock? When do you need to bounce back? Some of the answers you found in Chapter I: Sharpen the REAL LEADER in you. How to bring your REAL SELF, your true self to work. As a leader, you make sure that you are working with and from your whole true REAL SELF as a leader. Why is being authentic so critical to resilience? When life is hard or any sort of disruption hits, you have a finite amount of energy to deal with it, and your mask might fall off. Values, passion, and living a purposeful and meaningful life will all help anchor you.

When you are grounded and anchored you create a circle of safety with your leadership presence. You come across as being fully present, level-headed, and calm. If you are not stable, even as you walk down the corridor, people can read you and sense that you are not in balance.

### Values

Your deeply rooted personal and company values should not only be presented in abstract forms but lived every day. Make sure you remind yourself what matters every day. This will ground you. This is your first rock.

### Passion

The second rock is your **passion** your fire. If what you do is not in line with your driving forces, sooner or later you will feel frustrated and out of balance.

This is why I profile leaders at the beginning of my work; we can quickly see where, how, and why they have a dissonance and erode their fuel, their energy.

### A purposeful and meaningful life

The third rock is living a purposeful and meaningful life. This is huge. It is hard to define what a purposeful and meaningful life means. As the leaders I interviewed mentioned, it is becoming increasingly important. It is "a deep belief that what you are doing is meaningful".

## Skilful energy management in mastering RESILIENCE

"Leaders are the stewards of organisational energy" (Loehr and Schwartz, 2003:5). Therefore, how you manage your energy budget is not only a service to yourself but an important service to your organisation. To avoid the burn-out and fatigue that comes from constant adaptation you must master the principles of skilful energy management. Performance, health, and happiness are based on the skilful management of energy. Energy is your most precious resource. You only have a certain amount of it. You need to choose wisely when and how to use it. It requires both self-awareness and self-discipline to decide when to give all, when to limit, and when to be conscious about your fuel emission.

Leaders who do not make time for self-care can harm themselves and their organisation. They can both inspire and demoralise others by how effectively they manage their own energy and how well they mobilise, focus, invest, and renew the collective energy of those they lead. According to Loehr and Schwartz (2003), the skilful management of energy happens at 4 levels: physical, emotional, mental, and spiritual. Individually and organisationally, this makes it possible to have the full engagement of people and to maintain a sustainable resilient organisation.

If you don't practise self-care, you may end up making poor business decisions, snap at employees, or experience physiological and psychological symptoms such as depression. You might gain weight and suffer from insomnia. You cannot take care of people if you don't take care of yourself. It is a bit like the safety briefing on aeroplanes: you must put the oxygen mask on yourself first before you help others. The resilient leader is physically energised, emotionally connected, mentally focused, and spiritually aligned with a purpose beyond immediate self-interest.

Did you know for example that decision-making consumes energy? Over time it can lead to fatigue and indecisiveness. As a leader, you need to make lots of decisions every day.

If you have been in an executive position for a long time, how do you revitalise and renew yourself? If you can't, or if you are not able, are you ready to recognise that? Remember, you have a great impact on your organisation, whether it is a positive one or a negative one.

## Principles of skilful energy management

There are 4 key energy management principles that are critical for building the capacity to live a productive and fully engaged life (Loehr and Schwartz, 2003). I think energy management is also the criterion for being resilient.

### *Principle #1*

Being fully engaged and resilient requires you to draw on 4 separate but related sources of energy: physical, emotional, mental, and spiritual (which is about being purposeful, a 'why' to live). When you recognise how each profoundly influences the others, it makes a difference.

### *Principle #2*

Energy capacity diminishes both with overuse (working long hours, being under pressure for a long period) and with underuse (apathy, neglecting your own why, your lack of passion). You must balance your energy expenditure with periodical energy renewal. You may rarely consider how much energy you are spending because you tend to take it for granted and wrongly assume that the energy available to you is limitless. But you are mistaken. Sound familiar? Are you running an endless marathon while doing sprints, pushing yourself beyond healthy levels of exertion? Do you flatline mentally and emotionally by relentlessly spending energy without sufficient recovery? Learn to live your life as a series of sprints – fully engaging for periods, then fully disengaging, and seeking renewal of energy at every level before jumping back to sprint again.

### *Principle #3*

To build capacity you must push beyond your normal limits, training in the same systematic way that elite athletes do. Interestingly, stress is not the enemy in your life. Paradoxically, it is the key to growth. To build strength in a muscle, you must systematically stress it, which literally causes microscopic tears in the muscle fibres. At the end of each training session, the functional capacity is diminished. But give the muscle 24 to 48 hours to recover and it grows stronger. Knowing this, you can build emotional, mental, and spiritual capacity in the same way as you build physical capacity.

### *Principle #4*

Positive energy rituals – highly specific routines for managing energy – are the key to full engagement and sustained high performance. Change and continuous adaptation are difficult. You are creatures of habit. Most of what you do is automatic and unconscious. The problem with most efforts at change is that conscious effort cannot be sustained in the long run. Therefore, to change, you need to use positive rituals (behaviour that becomes automatic over time) fuelled by some deeply held values. The power of rituals is that they ensure that you use as little conscious energy as possible where it is not absolutely necessary, leaving you free to focus the energy available to you strategically in creative and enriching ways. As Will Durant said, "We are what we repeatedly do" (Durrant, 1991).

Many leaders push themselves beyond normal limits without intentional recovery routines. Therefore, remember energy is your most precious resource. It's a balancing act between expenditure and recovery of energy (sprints and recovery).

"Most athletes spend about 90% of their time training to be able to perform at peak levels 10% of the time. Business leaders are expected to perform 90% of the time with much less than 10% of their time spent on training or recovery. It appears that the most overworked athlete in the world is the corporate executive. As a result, leaders become burned out, making them less able to withstand disruption with strikes" (Eggers and Barlow, 2019:27).

### Reflection points

- As a leader, how valuable would it be to bring more positive energy and passion to your organisation?
- If those you lead would bring more positive energy into the workplace, how would it affect their relationships with their colleagues and the quality of service that they deliver to customers and clients?

Every thought, feeling, and action has an energy consequence. How you manage it makes you more or less resilient as a leader. Let's explore all 4 energy sources in detail.

## Physical energy

It is fundamental to be physically energised because it is the fuel for any human. Many of us run on an empty tank without the ability to expand and recover energy at the physical level. "Too much energy expenditure without sufficient recovery eventually leads to burnout and breakdown (overuse it and lose it). Too much recovery without sufficient stress leads to atrophy and weakness (use it or lose it)" (Loehr and Schwartz, 2003:29).

**Figure 4.1: Measuring the quantity of physical energy on a scale of 1 to 10 (Amended from source: Loehr and Schwartz, 2003).**

Physical energy is measured by the quantity of energy (Figure 4.1). The metric is low or high on your physical energy scale. I usually ask my executive clients how energised they feel physically on a scale of 1 to 10:1 is low, feeling physically flat; 10 is highly energised. When my clients state the number (let's say it's 5), I usually ask what it means? Why do they feel 5? What is going on? Then we discuss how the number can be increased. Of course, there is a goal related to this but moving to the actions first, clients need to face the truth about their responsibility for it. They may be neglecting this area, and therefore, letting themselves down. They must take full ownership. Blame needs to go; whether the object of the blame is something far-fetched or abstract like time or having too many tasks, it must go.

Physical energy is derived from the patterns of our breathing, the food that we eat, the quantity and quality of our sleep, to what extent and what kind of energy recovery sessions we implement into our day and at what level our fitness is.

The sources of physical energy are breathing, fitness, diet, sleep, rest, and hydration. These are the most important sources of recovery in your life.

## Emotional energy

Emotional capacity is reflected in our ability to expand and recover energy at the emotional level and be emotionally connected. We need a real connection with openness without judgement, without assumptions. We need to actively listen and empathise, to be curious about the person we are talking to. Emotional energy is measured by the quality of our energy (Figure 4.2).

**Figure 4.2: Measuring the quality of emotional energy on a scale of 1 to 10 (Amended from source: Loehr and Schwartz, 2003).**

The metric is negative or positive. Again, I use scaling here with my clients and ask how they feel on a scale of 1 to 10, where 1 is feeling really negative (anger, fear, sadness, etc.) and 10 feel really positive (love, joy, excitement, etc.). I ask how they feel most of the time at work and in life generally? When they say the number, we talk about what it means, about whether it fluctuates. We also look at what kinds of events influence the emotional energy of the person? And finally, what can be done to move higher on the scale.

The sources of emotional energy are caring, compassion, confidence, enjoyment, gratitude, and challenge.

## Mental energy

We will talk about being mentally focused at length in Chapter V: F is for FOCUS and explore another dimension of mental capacity and energy in Chapter IV: A is for AGILITY, when we discuss brain fitness (whole-brain functioning), which impacts cognitive ability.

Limited mental capacity is when we are mentally absent, when we are checked out mentally and mentally disengaged. We measure mental energy by the focus of energy. The metric is broad or narrow depending on our focus, presented again on a scale (Figure 4.3).

**Figure 4.3: Measuring the focus of mental energy on a scale of 1 to 10 (Amended from source: Loehr and Schwartz, 2003).**

We derive mental energy from our thinking process and thinking capacity, from mastering leadership focus, and from achieving flexibility in our thinking and focus.

## Spiritual energy

Being spiritually aligned means knowing our why and our company's why. This is very complex as it contains synergy among shifting forces, from me to we (from self to others), from external to internal (being centred and aligned with our higher purpose) and from negative to positive. Where we stand on this complex scale means how much we are aligned and how much we live a purposeful, meaningful life (Figure 4.4).

**Figure 4.4: Measuring shifts in spiritual energy on a scale of 1 to 10 (Amended from source: Loehr and Schwartz, 2003).**

The sources of spiritual energy are integrity, honesty, courage, persistence, passion, commitment, and service to others.

There exists a dynamic relationship between physical, emotional, mental, and spiritual energy. As one leader noted:

> "Being resilient at a systemic level is like Aikido, the martial arts, how an organisation can use the energy of their environment, of all the forces in a wider context, e.g., current global and industrial trends."

According to Loehr and Schwarz (2003), there is a development line, a particular sequence followed in effective energy management (Figure 4.5).

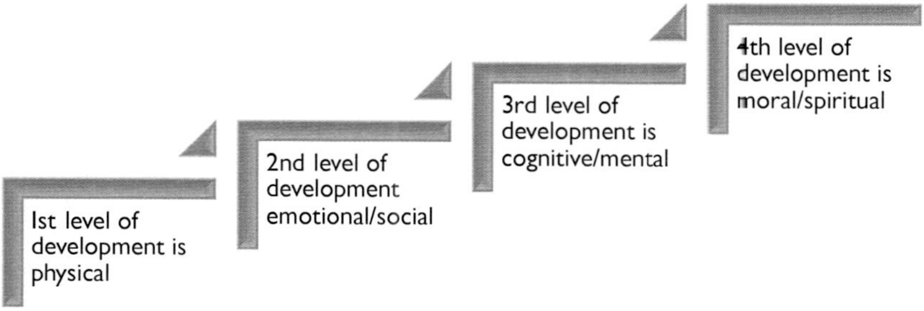


**Figure 4.5: The sequence of effective energy management (Loehr and Schwartz, 2003).**

A daily practice of 90 to 120 minutes of intensive effort followed by shorter periods of recovery and renewal of energy is a must for effective energy management and to prevent leaders from burnout and fatigue. Research has proven that the world's best athletes all build highly structured recovery routines into their lives (Loehr and Schwartz, 2003).

As I mentioned before, leaders can both inspire and demoralise others by how effectively they manage their own energy and how well they mobilise, focus, invest, and renew the collective energy of those they lead.

Think about it. How much time do you spend on your organisation's financial budget each year? A lot, right? And how much time do you spend on your own energy budget? On your organisation's energy budget?

### Reflection points

- To deliver high performance, to bring out the best in you and perform at your maximum level for an extended period, you need lots of energy. As a leader, how do you take control of your energy budget?
- Where do you leak energy and where do you gain energy during work?
- How are you spending your energy now?
- How can you keep performing at your best without sacrificing your health, your happiness, and your passion for life?

- In which of the 4 areas (physical, emotional, mental, and spiritual) do you feel the most deficit?
- What does your energy budget look like? When was the last time you considered whether you were overusing or underusing your energy capacity?

## Leadership insights

"When the pandemic hit, many leaders introduced restrictions and rules, which limited the room for manoeuvring for their people. I did it the other way around. I let them bring ideas about how to tackle the crisis and gave them space. I trusted the flexibility and creativity of the team."

"Resilience is more holistic. It is about being resilient at the mental and physical levels as well. Smoking less, eating healthily, and doing movements regularly. We introduced a company programme into the organisation, which has impacted everyone at the organisation not only while they are at work but in their everyday life generally. We set a monthly challenge of running 50 km. We created a FB group to support each other in this challenge. We even went further and announced that we have a social responsibility here. I feel I have an impact on their life even if I am not with them. Of course, not everyone liked it. But I was very committed. If they can live their retirement days one year longer, and if I contributed to that, it is a great feeling."

"I can be creative, resilient, and agile, but if I don't pay attention to where my organisation stands, my high level of resilience, creativity, and agility has zero value. I need to be aware of the impact I make with these. I make sure they can keep up with me. And here HR and Training can help me a lot. The level of pressure is relative. There are many levels. The important thing for me is not to be crushed under a high level of stress and pressure. To see the way forward, not to get panicked and fall into despair. I don't think we have to make crisis plans right away; instead, we should look for a way out."

# CHAPTER IV

# A is for AGILITY

"In the new world,
it is not the big fish which eats the small fish,
it's the fast fish which eats the slow fish."

(Klaus Schwab, 2015)

## The meaning of AGILITY

Agility is defined in the Oxford English Dictionary (2021) as the "ability to move and respond quickly and easily" and the "ability to think and understand quickly". This response is more proactive than reactive. Agility is not just about a proactive response, i.e., creating things before they appear; it is also about eliminating them. Although, when we deal with agility, we must remind ourselves that "agility is the means, not the end" (Hayward, 2018:14). Otherwise, "we may end up with an agile hammer, and start seeing agile nails everywhere" as one of the leaders I interviewed put it. Another described it thus:

> "As if you were on the battlefield: it does not matter if you stand still or go straight ahead because you can easily become a target in either way. If you are changing the direction, the pace, the speed,

> and the tactics, but you are still going towards the chosen building, you have already become a hard target. And that is agility for me."

I found from the interviews that the common features of agility are about moving fast; a quick response to the rapidly changing environment is required. Many leaders described it as a trendy topic and a buzzword. Some said that it is very much under their skin, which means that there is a high level of penetration and knowledge of agility within their organisation. Others again thought that it didn't apply to them, and therefore, couldn't be implemented as a whole, or they strongly held the view that you shouldn't throw a trendy concept into the organisation without thinking it through carefully. However, they all agreed that agility requires quick thinking, proactive behaviour, and readiness in terms of anticipating future needs to be able to prepare themselves and their organisation for rapid movements and changes pointing forward. One in particular noted:

> "Agility for me is not the same thing as making a hasty decision, because that is pure judgement from the leader's side. For me, when agility comes to mind, first I think of flexibility rather than speed."

Interestingly, many leaders said that for them CREATIVITY, RESILIENCE, FOCUS, and TRUST, together create the premise for AGILITY, which are in fact the qualities of CRAFT Leadership. How surprising?!

## Why AGILITY matters so much today

In our digital and politically unpredictable world, agility has never been more relevant in leadership, because of the continuous changes occurring in today's organisations and markets. Adaptability, agility, and flexibility have become increasingly important to ensure the future progress of organisations and people and their unremitting performance improvement. Organisations are only as agile as the people who work for them; people make the organisation what it is.

The pressure from fears of becoming out-dated, missing business opportunities to the benefit of the competitors in the fast-paced VUCA world, and change and disruption are becoming commonplace, the norm. Leaders, therefore, need to be able to do things quickly; they need to be able to pivot regularly, meaning they will need to be AGILE.

"Organisations should respond quickly to emerging threats and challenges so being able to move quickly and easily they need a strong spine and supple muscles," says Hayward (2018:4). At the edge of chaos and complexity, leaders need to create clarity and stability while moving at a speed of 300 km/hour. They must sharpen their leadership quality of being able to respond to unexpected opportunities or threats with speed and accuracy.

In this chapter, rather than talking about the agile ways of working, the agile frameworks, like scrums and lean methodologies, etc., we'll approach agility in a much more fundamental way.

Across all sectors, boards increasingly reward executives for their ability to grow their business despite the high levels of uncertainty and ambiguity that come with fast-paced change. This is where agility comes in, as a capability for unleashing inner entrepreneurship with a high survival mechanism of delivering results no matter what and adapting more flexibly to uncertainty. Thus, to remain competitive in the market leaders must deliver results. They have to be adaptable and flexible and be able to renew themselves and their organisation. The latter two cannot be achieved without mastering agility.

Mastering agility means being able to learn, unlearn, and relearn. The very basics of all these lie in Neuro-Agility.

Creating greater organisational agility is one of the top concerns of chief executives. How swiftly can they respond to the needs of the business to prosper? There is no agile business, agile organisational structure, or agile business operation without agile people and agile leaders. They can enhance organisational agility without implementing any agile methodology. In fact, some of the leaders I interviewed talked about agility by naming it, or they described the characteristics of agility as present or future demand for their organisation without considering implementing the methodology itself.

## Leadership insights

"Last year was extremely hard, I completely forgot how not to be agile."

"The world has accelerated almost banally; the hustle and bustle have become trendy. Although agility is said to be important for survival today, if we spin more, we will not necessarily achieve progress any better or faster. How do we measure it? The fundamental things have really not changed. When I see a colleague who is running with a folder in their hand in the corridor, I don't necessarily think they are more productive. Look, the other day I watched a movie from the 70s. It started slowly. The first 15 minutes were slow, I mean really, really slow, but by the end, it turned out to be a thrilling and rather complex story. I enjoyed it immensely! Compared to another movie, called *Mission Impossible*, in which 10 people died in the first 3 or 4 minutes, it was full of action, with impressive movie effects, but you know what, in the end, I had no clue what it was about. So, what I am trying to say here is that we shouldn't become agile for the sake of agility, because it can hide the real problems. We have to ask ourselves the very question: What is the purpose? What do we want to achieve with this?"

"There was an area in my business where one senior manager and one director left the company at the same time. I decided not to hire such expensive people from the labour market but handed their tasks over to two younger and less experienced people from my team. I stood by them. I supported them with leadership agility and made them work in a rather unconventional way. They grew up and grew into those positions within a year. I was always there for them. I taught them how to think in an agile way. When they came to see me with their agenda, I interrupted them, and didn't let them follow through. Instead, I challenged them, probed them with questions and as a result, I made them fly in totally new directions, to new lands. I deliberately left them there to see if they could fly home alone. Consequently, these overly structured and rigid people have learnt how to be agile and flexible. But this is a learned behaviour for them."

"A leader must be brave and agile enough to open people's eyes, to deviate from the usual patterns, to challenge the status quo. We can be more ambitious. Sometimes we only see the goal, but the breakdown of the path to the goal is not so clear. In a world full of disruptions, we often run from wall to wall. But recognising that sometimes we have to speed up and sometimes we have to slow down on that path, this is also a matter of agility."

It is important to see how and in what way agility can bring value to leadership and how and in what way it can become counterproductive and go against fundamentals. As one of the leaders pointed out:

> "A child cannot be born within one month by 9 women, because all 9 women will generally need 9 months to carry a child to term."

In this chapter, I will share how I approach agility with my executive clients. We'll talk about the key attributes and characteristics of agile leadership and then look into where agility as a leadership quality starts from and how you can build on this. To give you something to take with you, we'll explore Neuro-Agility and a two-part tool: 1) 7 elements of your unique neuro-design and 2) 6 drivers to optimise and enhance your Neuro-Agility and overall flexibility.

## The agile leader

According to Hayward (2018), an agile leader has 4 attributes:

- learning agility (enabler)
- empathy (enabler)
- thoughtful decisiveness (disruptor)
- digital literacy (disruptor)

He goes on to say that leaders need to embrace the paradox of agile leadership to be agile. They should bring both their enabler and disruptor sides to the table to shake up ways of thinking, embrace ideas from different perspectives, and link unrelated pieces of information together to see new possibilities and challenge the status quo. It is a balancing act. Agile leaders are both connected and connecting leaders. They are both enablers and disruptors at the same time.

- **Enablers:** learning agility, giving clear directions, empathising and trusting, empowering, working together.
- **Disruptors**: thoughtfully decisive, digitally literate, questioning and challenging the status quo, creating new ways of thinking, close to customer trends, taking risks to find new ways of providing services.

### *What does agility look like in leadership? 20 characteristics of being an agile leader:*

1. **Adaptive thinker:** Think more adaptively, and integrate new creative ways of thinking. A regional managing director I spoke to put it like this:

   "My problem is that training courses always give recipes. Being agile does not mean you follow recipes. It always depends on impulses and being very adaptive."

2. **Disrupts**: Disrupt yourself before you disrupt your organisation. If you miss taking control of disruption you will end up being disrupted, which results in your being more reactive than proactive.

3. **Future-focused:** See more and before (Maxwell, 2018) by constantly reading the business landscape of today and tomorrow. Being future-forward and proactive means that you do not wait for the needs to arrive; rather you create the needs.

4. **Connected and connecting**: Be more connected at many levels and in many directions, such as internal and external, up and down, horizontal and vertical, and so on. Get and stay close to your customers. Promote cross-functional, cross-industry collaboration and co-creation across organisations geographically with partners, customers, and suppliers.

5. **Has a range of perspectives:** Embrace diversity to gain and reach a greater choice of perspectives. Invite a more diversified group of stakeholders to the table including non-customers who could be potential future customers, non-profit organisations with social responsibilities, or competitors for that matter. Explicitly welcome differences and build complementary and expanded teams.

6. **Possibility thinker**: Challenge the status quo regularly. Don't rely on tried and tested methods. Be courageous to embrace radical possibilities. Be optimistic and confident about the future.

7. **Outcome-focused**: Cut through the bureaucracy. Reduce the level of regulation and re-imagine the business operating model with simplification and smart controls. As one of the interviewed leaders put it:

   "Don't overregulate your people; instead expect outputs from them."

8. **Uses a one-firm approach**: Smash silos and challenge tribal thinking. Advocate the one-firm approach. Once I conducted a *One-Firm Approach to Business Development Program Series* for the whole leadership and management team of an organisation. I was surprised to see how smart and talented people stayed in the bubble of their own expertise and found it uncomfortable and even challenging to come up with questions for their clients that were beyond their defined bubbles. As we explored in Chapter II: C is for CREATIVITY and CREATE, tapping into your curiosity takes you out of your bubble and pushes your interest in others.

9. **Embraces continuous development**: Encourage people and role model failing and learning from mistakes. Don't just inspire others by your own discovery journey but show them how to be disciplined and intentional in their development. One leader noted:

   "There must be a constant need for development. How quickly and strongly do we want and are we able to implement it? 'I'm very agile' says someone, but if we look back and review their performance, they have barely changed; they are not agile at all."

10. **Provides clarity:** Constantly communicate on where your organisation is heading and what key long-term priorities are important.

11. **Promotes a feedback culture**: Promote a feedback culture and create shorter feedback loops to fail fast and early and learn fast.

12. **Innovates:** Stimulate innovation and creativity by creating an environment for generating new ideas.

13. **Simplifies**: Focus on and drive simplicity. Carry out activities in the shortest possible time. Reduce complexity.

14. **Encourages experimentation and failing-forward**: Encourage constant learning by creating a safe environment in which it is allowed to make mistakes. Not only promote but also role model continuous improvement by admitting mistakes and getting better every day. The improvements link to milestones with a feedback and correction process. The agile leader recognises that these projects are not organised along a hierarchy but based on motivation, knowledge, and strengths.

15. **Uses change muscles:** Adapt quickly and flexibly in response to change in the external environment, and to the complex needs of customers and different stakeholders. As one of the interviewed leaders put it:

    "Leaders should be able to solve the Rubik's cube fast today."

    The mode, direction, and speed of response determine how agile you and your organisation are.

16. **Value-driven**: Find new ways to create values for customers and people. Build a value-based organisation that can give stability to the organisation to tackle future, yet unseen challenges. As one of the interviewed SME managing directors put it:

    "We need to have a set of values in place that makes the community itself resilient and agile as they go hand in hand. For us, they are safety, respect, and trust. Every human being wants safety, everyone enjoys and flourishes in a trustful environment, and everyone longs for being respected just because they are a human being."

    If you are a good agile leader, you are a value-based leader, who can change flexibly on the go. It is important not to pull the company right and left. It is not the goals that are the most important but the values. As a value-based agile leader, you are willing to change and can easily change quickly and flexibly the short-term solutions. This makes you adaptable.

17. **Prioritises**: Prioritisation is at the heart of agility. It is about making difficult choices, cutting out irrelevant things, and doing the few most important things. Also, aligned priorities at the organisational level reduce internal conflicts.

18. **Empowers:** Empower others to take ownership and make decisions. Allow the people who are closest to the customers, the richest sources of information, to make decisions. Give them the autonomy and the authority to make decisions because they are the most aware of the context of the situation and they have the competence to take the best actions. Decentralisation is highly important in an agile operation.

    "Entrust the decision to those who understand the problem best, empower them, but don't give them specific tools. Instead, give them a toolkit (make them resourceful) and let them choose what to use and how to use it."

19. **Gives up (some) control:** Or rather, as an agile leader, you create minimum control and build trust in which you allow your team to be more self-organised.

20. **Re-constructs boundaries:** Challenge and push boundaries and find new ways to do things.

---

## Leadership insights

"You are agile if you give value to the customer on the go, if you create value outside your walls so quickly and efficiently that the loss of constant change is less than the extra value you can produce. This is how I define being effective or agile. What if we invest in something that makes an organisation's agility cheaper? If it is developed for and by someone closer to the customer, who understands the customer, who can communicate with the customer? Developers can't do this. I can anticipate what the future needs will be. And then we have created a platform that includes not only solutions for current needs but future needs, as well. It can be used by customer service. So, we don't have to go to developers all the time, which would make the whole process much slower. This is how customer service can quickly and effectively respond to the new needs of the client while being on the phone call with them. The clients' feedback was priceless!"

"I'm a horribly impatient person. It's very important for me to react quickly. Something always happens in the book market every day. If you don't keep an eye on things, you can easily fall behind. We need to be sharp to see what we need to take from the changes, to be able to ride the waves of change."

### Reflection points

The definition of being agile differs for each team as they are very different in the various businesses. And agility differs for every organisation.

- What does agility mean for you, for your team, and for your organisation?
- Why is agility important (if so) and how can you make it happen as a leader?
- What is your role as a leader in it?

On that note have a look at each item on the Agile Leader Characteristics list. Mark those that you know for sure constitute an integral part of your leadership. Write down pieces of evidence, meaning two concrete examples for each item you've marked. Be as detailed and specific as possible. Then have a look at those that are not part of your leadership, i.e., the ones you have not marked.

- How many are on the second list?
- To what extent do you need to develop them and how can they help you lead your organisation from good to great?
- What can you do to start implementing them?

Commit to 3–4 small action points and follow them through.

## AGILITY starts with thinking

There are 3 stages of agile thinking: perception, reaction, and execution (Cox, 2002):

1. **Perception**: We sense or anticipate the stimulus, read the situation, and make sense of what it means for us.
2. **Reaction**: We interpret the stimulus and choose what to do.
3. **Execution:** We initiate the response.

In this cognitive (and also physical) activity, speed is key.

Everything starts with thinking. Once we are thinking with agility, we can believe in an agile way. Agility is both mental and physical. The speed of processing is key to how agile we are. Neuro-Agility and brain fitness help in this arena. One leader interviewed put it nicely:

> "Learning agility is the only sustainable competitive advantage for the future."

The only way to out-perform, to out-create your competitors is if you out-think and out-learn them. So, once you are agile in your thinking, you can behave in an agile way, but this takes a lot of effort, fuel, and energy. This can be hard; therefore, resilience is the supporting sister of agility. Slow down in order to speed up.

## Working with AGILITY – The power of Neuro-Agility

The only way people and businesses will maintain a competitive advantage in this rapidly changing, information-soaked, turbulent world is to be able to out-think, out-learn and out-create any competition. Learning is the DNA of the mind. By gaining deep insight into how the brain functions in support of learning, critical thinking, creativity, problem-solving, neuroplasticity, and decisionmaking, we can better prepare people to adapt to, and prepare for a continually changing marketplace, thus allowing companies to maintain a competitive advantage. It is a holistic approach.

Agile brainpower can help people do things simpler, better, and faster. Understanding and learning what we can do to make our brain work faster and more effectively is key. According to both the 10th PwC CEO's Survey (2021) in Hungary and global leaders, the leaders' No. 1 focus area to achieve corporate growth or profitability is seeking operational effectiveness. Do more with less (fewer people, less time), i.e., do things simpler, better, and faster. In organisations today, we talk more about agile operations and processes and less about agile people and agile behaviours. How can people become more agile?

### *Why brain agility is important*

According to Arie de Geus (1988) "The ability to learn faster than competitors may be the only sustainable competitive advantage."

Neuroscience tells us that our brain has unlimited potential, so there is no limitation to who you can become if you understand, develop, and utilise your unique brainpower.

Also, half of the future skills needed to thrive in the Fourth Industrial Revolution mentioned by the World Economic Forum (2020) are brainpower skills: analytical thinking and innovation; complex problem solving; critical thinking and analysis; creativity, originality, and initiative; and reasoning, problem-solving, and ideation. In the past, cognitive flexibility was part of future skills. It still is, but they rename this category to include resilience, stress tolerance, and overall flexibility.

The designer and founder of Neuro-Agility, Dr André Vermeulen (2018) says: "Knowing your unique neurological design and understanding the 6 drivers that impact this is the key to Neuro-Agility, talent development, and performance improvement."

### *What is Neuro-Agility?*

Vermeulen (2018) describes Neuro-Agility as "the readiness of the senses and brain regions to function as one integrated whole brain system, being receptive and responsive to receive and transmit bio-chemical impulses at optimal capacity under new and potential stress conditions. People who are highly neuro-agile have the flexibility to learn new skills, attitudes and behaviours fast and easy and unlearn old-behaviour patterns quickly."

A leader with an agile brain can learn new skills faster and cope with stress better than one with an unfit brain. Neuro-Agility prepares leaders for the future and its disruptive changes; it trains them to out-think, out-learn, and out-perform machines.

### *Rewire and sharpen your thinking processes in uncertainties*

If you've been going through a business transformation, your people will need to be as agile as your processes. Deal with agility and flexibility on the most fundamental level. Increasing the agile brainpower of every individual, leader, and the team will help you reduce the cost of change and enable them to think faster and more innovatively, learn faster and perform better.

### *Neuro-Agility Profile™ for leaders*

Neuro-Agility is about optimising the brain-based elements that influence the ease, speed, and flexibility with which you think, learn, and process information in today's complex business environment.

Developing and optimising these elements are the starting point to improve your fitness and mental flexibility in order to thrive and be employable, successful, and effective in a VUCA world.

RENEWAL OF SELF and FLEXIBILITY are two of the key success factors of leadership.

## Did you know?

- Today, our brain processes 30 times more information than it did 20 years ago.
- 75% to 90% of diseases due to stress are related to information overload.
- We are reading less, and we are reading slower; our ability to concentrate lasts for 15 to 20 minutes or even less.
- We forget 90% of what we learn in a week.
- Electronic devices think for us.

You cannot ignore the fact that you must prepare yourself as a leader to keep up with the speed of change. There is no limitation to who you can become if you understand, develop, and utilise your unique brainpower. Utilise your whole brain in such a way that you can come up with innovative ideas and produce better results than your competitors.

People who are highly neuro-agile have the flexibility to learn new skills, attitudes, and behaviours quickly and easily, and unlearn old behaviour patterns quickly, too. They possess sharp cognitive agility, which means they are always looking for answers, believing they can find them. They are convinced that there is more than one solution to any problem. They do not only see the problems here and now but have the flexibility to zoom out and see them from a big picture perspective. They anticipate and envision future challenges and work on the readiness of their organisation to be prepared for those future challenges.

### *Business benefits of Neuro-Agility Profile™*

Effective and successful leaders have an accurate awareness of their learning and thinking preferences. The Neuro-Agility Profile™ led by Dr André Vermeulen and developed by Neuro-Link Global has many advantages for you in the development of this leadership quality (Vermeulen, 2018):

- Obtain accurate awareness of your untapped potential.
- Understand how you are talented and smart because this is where you show high energy and passion.
- Increase your mental and cognitive flexibility and overall adaptability.
- Become more agile in your thinking and learning.

- Optimise your overall brain fitness.
- Strengthen your brain health.
- Accelerate brainpower skills like complex problem solving, and critical and creative thinking.
- Cope with stress and fatigue more effectively.
- Achieve a better work/life balance.
- Develop a growth mindset.

### *7 components of unique neurological design*

People's neurological design is as unique as their fingerprints. Vermeulen uses 7 factors to show how each of us is uniquely wired. He believes all people are talented but in different ways. Some may be more talented than others, but they all have talents (Figure 5.1).

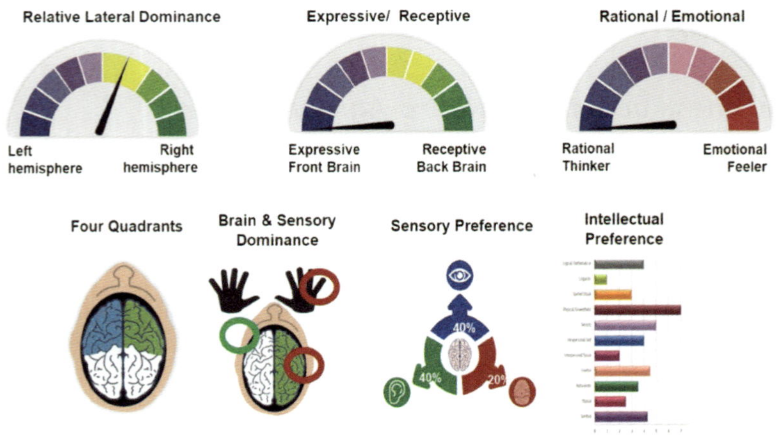


**Figure 5.1: Example dashboard of the 7 Factors that Impact Our Neurological Design (Vermeulen, 2018).**

1. **Relative lateral dominance:** Are you dominantly using the left or right hemisphere of your brain? The left-brain hemisphere is the logical, analytical, or language hemisphere. The right-brain

hemisphere is the creative and holistic hemisphere. Although we use both hemispheres, one always leads (the dominant side) and the other follows. Under stress and fatigue the one that follows switches off. The dominant side is genetically determined. The aim is to be and work bilaterally by activating both sides of your brain.

2. **Expressive/receptive:** Do you use more of your front brain (expressive learner) or back brain (receptive learner)? If you are more expressive, you are more verbally oriented, and more outspoken. You can easily express your thoughts and feelings through language. If you are more receptive, you are more reserved and think before you act. You are a reflecting and absorbing learner. Under stress and fatigue, you either tend to become more talkative, less listening (expressive) or shy, quiet, and don't give voice to your opinions. The aim for you is to develop and maintain a balance between talking and participating, and listening and observing.

3. **Rational/emotional:** Are you more of a thinking person or a feeling person? Do you use more of the cerebral area, the outside layer of your brain, or the limbic system/deeper inside area of your brain? If you are emotional you tend to express your emotions spontaneously by talking, laughing, shouting, etc., or getting angry when under stress, spontaneously reacting. Often your emotions may dominate your rational thoughts. If you are rational you tend to be more factual and objective and think things through before reacting. Under stress you overly rationalise things.

4. **Four quadrants of the brain:** Which quadrant of the cerebral cortex do you prefer to use? The 4 profiles illustrate the unique sequence of how you prefer to use your whole brain in everyday situations. This profile clarifies what role you prefer to play. You can be a strategist, an analyst, a counsellor, and a doer. You can approach tasks in your unique sequence, i.e., starting as a strategist with the big-picture thinking, then filling in the details as an analyst, then starting to think about with whom and how you should resource your project by switching on your counsellor side, and finally it is time for you to start execution as a doer.
5. **Brain and sensory dominance:** How do you genetically process information? Did you know that the left hemisphere controls your senses on the right side of your body (right hand, right eye, and right ear), while the right hemisphere controls your senses on the left side of your body (left hand, left eye, and left ear)? There are 16 unique dominance profile combinations in the processing function. If you have uniform dominance (no sense hinders you in processing information) you're not at risk of human error when under stress. If you have mixed dominance (i.e., 1 or 2 senses are a hindrance) you have a low or moderate risk for human error when under stress. If you have blocked dominance genetically (i.e., 3 senses hinder how you process information) you are at high risk for human error when under stress.
6. **Sensory preference:** What percentage of your visual (illustrations, pictures, textbooks, diagrams, patterns), auditory (instructions, music, sounds, words), and kinaesthetic (moving, touching, doing, actions) senses do you use in your learning and thinking?

7. **Intellectual preference:** How smart are you? Vermeulen (2018) identified 11 intelligence preferences that show how smart people are and how they prefer to think and learn (logical, linguistic, visual, physical, sensory, intrapersonal, interpersonal, creative, naturalistic, musical, spiritual). When there is an alignment between intelligence preferences, subjects, and career choices, people become passionate about life and the work that they do. For example, creative/innovative intelligence is the ability to think in new ways, generate original ideas, and look at things from different angles. Most inventors and many entrepreneurs, like Thomas Edison and Richard Branson prefer this. It is important to know that it is not a competence, it is a preference.

Using the profile you can learn your Neuro-Design Flexibility Score, i.e., how you are wired and what level of flexibility you have.

### *6 drivers to optimise your brain performance*

All people have potential. Your brain has unlimited potential in terms of what you can learn, think, and create. To tap into this potential, you'll need to optimise your brain performance and enable all regions of your brain to function as a whole system. For this to happen, you need to create the right conditions. Figure 5.2 shows the 6 drivers that can help you impact your flexibility and unleash your potential (Vermeulen, 2018).

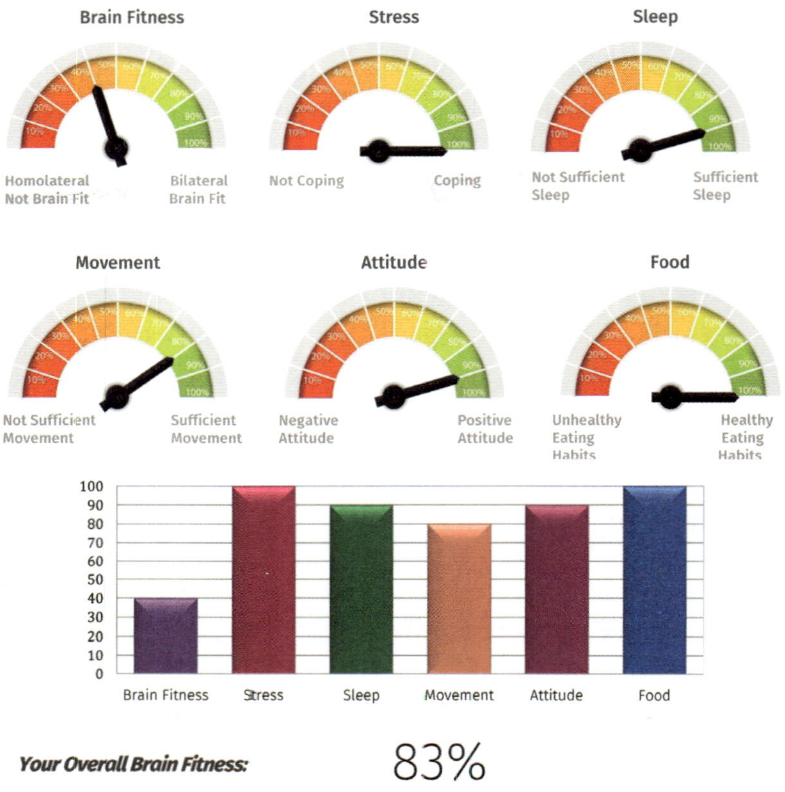


**Figure 5.2: Example of a brain-optimising dashboard, which contains the 6 drivers to optimise your brain performance (Vermeulen, 2018).**

What can you do to optimise your brain performance and become more agile?

1. **Brain fitness:** How do you use your brain hemispheres? In a one-sided or homolateral or two-sided, bilateral manner? Research shows that the average brain fitness of people is 48%, while ideally, you want to be nearer to 80% of brain fitness (Vermeulen, 2018). As far as the whole-brain approach is concerned: "C-Suite teams that proactively embrace and promote whole-brain approaches in their companies yield

better financial outcomes than those that don't" (Accenture, 2019). Accenture's research showed that only 8% of leaders use the whole-brain approach. C-suite leaders using a whole-brain approach to leadership are already seeing the positive bottom-line impact today, for example, stronger average growth and profitability (they realise +22% on average as per 3-year revenue growth and +34% on average as per 3-year profit (EBIDTA) growth). The aim is to utilise all brain regions simultaneously as one functional integrated system. There are several ways you can stimulate whole-brain functioning, for example, cross-lateral exercises, mental exercises, and stretching.

2. **Stress:** How does stress impact your brain's performance? Stress is the brain's worst enemy; it stimulates chemicals that inhibit the electrical transmission of impulses between brain cells. It can cause the non-dominant hemisphere to switch off while releasing cortisol in your body due to stress and anxiety. Cortisol is an inhibiting chemical that blocks the connection and transmission between neurons. When this happens, there is no learning, and the non-dominant hemisphere switches off. There are always opposing forces that create tension. As a leader, you need to learn how to live with this. Having a stress-coping mechanism in place is essential. There is another CRAFT Leadership quality (RESILIENCE) that plays an important role in managing stress. It is about how equipped you are to handle difficult situations. Some examples of how to cope with stress are stress relief breathing, relaxation, exercise, and humour.

3. **Sleep:** During sleep, your body system produces neurotransmitters that work not only for your happiness and healing, but also to create new connections and repair damaged cells. It is essential for you to learn how much you sleep and what quality of sleep you have and based on that how your sleep impacts your brain performance. Did you know that an hour's sleep before midnight is worth 2 hours after midnight (Vermeulen, 2018)?
4. **Movement:** Movement is the door to learning. How much movement (exercise, walking, swimming, etc.) do you have in your life? If you don't exercise sufficiently your brain's health and performance will be limited. Cross movements can help you activate all parts of your brain. When you exercise, it increases your oxygen intake. Oxygenated blood energises your brain and improves concentration. During exercise, your body produces neurotransmitters called endorphins, known as the happiness hormone, that strengthen your immune system and make you feel good. Don't underestimate its importance!
5. **Attitude:** Imagine that you can measure negative and positive attitudes on a scale. Where do you stand on that scale? Henry Ford is reputed to have said: "Whether you think you can or you can't ... you are right." A positive attitude is about possibility thinking, seeing possibilities, and appreciating what you have, expressing gratitude for small and ordinary things. It's 'the sun is always shining above the clouds' attitude. In our consumer society, the never-enough, the bigger-the-better, and the more-and-more attitudes go against an everyday positive attitude, leaving us unfulfilled. A leader is an enthusiast. You can only inspire others if you are inspired. Therefore, enthusiasm starts

with you as a leader. One of my clients says he goes for it, and this 'going the extra miles attitude comes from his belief that it's all in his mind.

6. **Food:** Your lifestyle and the food you eat have a direct influence on your information-processing ability, emotions, health, concentration, and how your brain performs. When asked by the Center for Creative Leadership (McDowell-Larsen, 2016), 75% of executives said their diet clearly impacted how they felt and performed. More and more scientific results show that food can and does have profound effects on the brain. Eating 5-6 servings per day of a variety of fruit and vegetables is the best way to provide your body with what it needs to produce antioxidants and nourish your brain. Berries, cherries, citrus fruit, dark leafy greens, broccoli, carrots, tomatoes, olives, fish, nuts, vitamin E, vitamin C, turmeric, green tea, onion, garlic, and cinnamon have all been shown to have beneficial effects, such as improving working memory, staving off or reversing cognitive decline, and increasing the ability to manage complex learning tasks. Studies also show that those using a Mediterranean style diet have a 33% lower risk of both cognitive impairment and Alzheimer's disease (McDowell-Larsen, 2016).

### Reflection points

- How do you think these drivers influence your brain health?
- How do you think these drivers impact your performance?
- In which areas do you still need to develop further?
- What is your plan of action to optimise your brain performance?

## Whole-brain leadership for agility

It is important to emphasise again that "C-Suite teams that proactively embrace and promote whole-brain approaches in their companies yield better financial outcomes than those that don't" (Accenture, 2019). Brainpower is our competitive advantage.

Today's employees are overwhelmed, distracted, and impatient. Being flexible about when, where, and how they learn is increasingly important. They want to learn from their peers, managers, and leaders, as much as from experts. And they are taking control of their own development. When it comes to learning, especially for experienced employees and leaders, the focus should not only be on how, when, and where they learn but on how and what they need to unlearn to be able to create space for new knowledge. Helping leaders become more flexible in the way they use their brains will support them to become more agile in the way they operate.

### Why leaders need to use their whole brain for optimum agility

For leaders to achieve competitive agility and solve complex business problems quickly and more productively, they need to learn how to use their whole brain (Accenture, 2019). Change requires leaders to assimilate data quickly (left, analytical hemisphere dominance) while simultaneously having the holistic intelligence to tap into the full potential of employees and consumers (right, creative hemisphere dominance). Leaders can learn how to access both sides of their brains simultaneously by learning how to become more neuro-agile and cognitively diverse – the most important skills for 2022 and beyond. To be fit for the future, leadership needs to be multi-dimensional to address the art and science of business. In today's business climate, focusing on growth, profitability, sustainability and improving trust, collaboration, and innovation are all important (Full Potential Group™, 2020).

Accenture (2019) confirms that 89% of C-suite leaders have formal training in left-brain-directed degrees with 65% admitting that a right-brain skill is their weakest one (empathy, self-awareness, coaching and empowering others, creative thinking, creating an inclusive team environment, intuition, etc.).

The neuro-plasticity of the brain proves we can all change and grow. Many great leadership programmes focus on helping leaders understand the power of mindset and how to change behaviours. The next step is to help leaders improve the flexibility and agility of their brains as the foundations for future growth, as well as expand their capacity for adaptability and continuous renewal required every day. Accenture's research (2019) shows that while only 8% of respondents use a whole-brain approach today, 82% intend to use a whole-brain approach in the next 3 years. Re-skilling leaders/C-suite members in whole-brain leadership and Neuro-Agility will create more possibilities to accelerate change and growth.

## Leadership insights

"Due to fast-changing technological advancement, we had to close down one of our competency fields and move into new areas. We had to downsize, but before laying off, we offered retraining and up-skilling for those people. We offered it to 100% of those who were affected. Out of that, only 70% took up our offer. But unfortunately, only 30%–40% were able to make it. These people were experienced generals with many stars, but they were transferred to a new area and lost their stars. I told them: 'You have no knowledge of this area, but you are clever, I trust you and I appreciate your hard work from the past, so I give you two stars for that.' They felt resentment and told me: 'Come on!' So, it was not only about their being unable to renew themselves (learn, unlearn, and relearn) but they had to fight and conquer their ego to make this shift. Only some of them were able to do it."

"They cannot let go of previously fixed things (patterns, routines, habits), and this causes the downfall of many agile organisations many times. They need to learn to let go of old habits. Because if we are doing the agile stuff right there is a natural 20%–30% of downsizing in it."

"A leader's role is to make their organisation somewhat lighter to free up some capacities to be able to quickly ride the waves of opportunities."

---

## Anecdote 5. My personal story with Neuro-Agility

Almost 3 years ago I embarked on a personal transformation journey. It was about changing a lifestyle. I started working with a personal trainer 4 times a week, I changed my dietary habits. I started taking better care of myself. In the middle of this journey in 2019, I came across the Neuro-Agility™ Profile tool. Completing the self-assessment test was part of my training and accreditation process. I was surprised to see the high scores (83% and 82%) I received on my brain-optimising and overall neuro-agility flexibility scores. I learnt at that time that this was way above average and generally it was an especially good scoring. It turned out that the change in my movement and dietary habits had had an enormous impact on my overall brain performance. When you introduce regular exercises into your life, you not only get fitter and slimmer, but you also feel happier. Exercise releases good chemicals in your body, which improves your mood. I have never come up with as many great ideas as when I was on the treadmill or the stationary bike. I also introduced backtasking (Chapter V: F is for FOCUS). It means that while I was doing cardio, I also listened to audiobooks and podcasts. So, when Vermeulen (2018) says "movement is a door to learning", he meant it. I also felt the constant release of positive hormones (serotonin, oxytocin, endorphins, dopamine) in my body. I felt invigorated, happier, and more positive. I saw more perspectives in my life than before. When you think positive thoughts, you produce neurotransmitters that facilitate thinking, learning, and creativity. Day after day I took deliberate actions to produce more facilitating neurotransmitter chemicals.

The other revelation I had was about food. I changed a lot regarding my dietary habits. I started to have 4 or 5, sometimes 6 meals per day. Before, I only had 3, sometimes 2. I started eating green vegetables and fruit mostly, and only chicken, turkey, and beef. I introduced more fish and seafood, berries, and nuts into my diet. I now drink a lot of green tea and water. I rarely drink alcohol and eat only complex carbohydrates with a low glycaemic index. Finally, I use only coconut and olive oil for cooking. Did you know that 2% of dehydration causes a 5% decrease in your brain capacity? These changes not only influenced my body shape, but I also realised that my thinking became sharper, and my complex problem-solving ability became more agile leaning. I became more proactive and more flexible and noticed that original ideas surface much easier. And above all, I know it will sound crazy, but my business development efforts skyrocketed with booming results, without the need to take any extra steps.

Experiencing, learning, and then working with this tool brings you a very holistic view and at the same time a scientific approach to developing your overall agility in a fundamental way.

Are you ready to see the castle in the pieces scattered around? Are you ready to sharpen the CRAFT Leadership quality of AGILITY?

# CHAPTER V

# F is for FOCUS

"How can you become the leader of few things
instead of the doer of many things?"

(Maxwell, 2015)

## Why FOCUS matters so much in leadership today

How hard or easy do leaders find it to stay focused? What challenges do they face when they are setting the focus and priorities for themselves and their organisations?

Leaders find it increasingly difficult to maintain focus nowadays. There is so much going on and so many things they need to take into consideration. Endless impulses and disruptions make their life much harder to control. The technology-driven VUCA world we live in creates too much noise, both internally and externally, where everything changes very quickly.

All of us suffer from information overload. We live our lives with crammed calendars. Big data is a blessing and a curse at the same time. As one of the leaders I interviewed pointed out:

> "I have neither the time nor the capacity to validate all the data available for me."

We have become information devourers. But do we need all of it? How much do we need to make good decisions, to be well informed, or informed enough to make the right decisions? The answer is not easy.

We live in an age of busyness where overworking, doing overtime, and going the extra mile are applauded. While we talk a lot about working smarter rather than harder, the latter is more incentivised. Globalisation opened our world, generating so many options, so many opportunities for both businesses and people. Leaders and executives end up working 60 hours per week as a norm. There is a saying in multinational organisations that the work cannot be finished/completed, it can only be stopped. How sad is this? It creates the feeling of being in a rat race, which results in burnout in many instances.

The challenges of today's business market are way too complex. This complexity expands the list of stakeholders for both leaders and organisations, bringing lots of contradicting and competing demands to the table for leaders to tackle. Finding the right or the best answer is sometimes very hard and, especially under enormous time pressure, it is even more challenging. In matrix organisations, there are many Key Performance Indicators (KPIs); often they are not aligned but pointing in many directions. This requires not only a laser-sharp focus but also the flexibility and the ability to see the details and the big picture at the same time and in the very instance.

## Today's challenges for leaders in FOCUS

All of us suffer from various challenges deriving from modern phenomena in today's society:

- **Information overload.** The tap is always open; it is almost impossible to switch it off.
- **Devouring information.** Today's easy access to all kinds of information via the internet has made us super consumers and addicted to more and more stimulants.
- **Multitasking.** We have a continuously increasing number of tasks on our plate. One of the leaders I worked with said he has a list of 40 tasks a day to handle, each of which requires anything from a couple of minutes to 20 or so hours. Another said he receives around 200 emails per day. It is insane and impossible to handle such an amount of work unless they have months, which I doubt. The long list of priorities (which frankly rob the word priority of its meaning) can paralyse people and cripple their life.
- **FOMO:** We have a fear of missing out, of being left out and left behind. We want to be involved in everything.
- **Action biased.** We are in a constant doing mode. And if we add speed to it, we are in a constant rushing mode.
- **Short-termism and impatience.** These are the king and queen of today's business environment. We want everything right now, this very instant. Leaders want management data and reports to be at their disposal with one click at first thought. Clients want a full customer experience with the first click and blink. Owners and shareholders demand quarterly results and returns on their investments no matter what. We live in an impatient world addicted to performance.

- **Dopamine.** According to Simon Sinek (2014), this instant gratification hormone has become the big boss and is fuelled by several sources. It contributes to the feeling of accomplishment and satisfaction we get from completing important tasks, achieving goals, or winning competitions. This is why checking a completed task off a list feels so-so good, even if it is a low-priority task. We want the positive feelings we get from dopamine. On the other hand, it enables us to stay focused, and get through difficult phases of our career, especially when we know where we want to go. However, it can be dangerous as well because it can lead to addictive behaviour. In a very goal-oriented and performance-driven organisation in which dopamine is the primary means of reward, we can easily become addicted, which can lead us to take on an uncontrollable workload without any boundaries.

Considering these phenomena combined, it's no wonder that there are so many leaders and managers (not to mention employees) who are burnt out after a couple of years in this business environment and that the engagement scores within the organisations are pretty low.

Having so many focus areas fragments our efforts, which leads to average performance or underperformance and a lack of a sense of fulfilment.

When I work with executives, I don't work with time management. No one can manage time. A day consists of 24 hours. That's it.

What I work with is FOCUS.

It is your choice as a leader to decide how to best use your efforts, to decide where you can bring the greatest value to your organisation and make the best out of the given time limit. In other words, where to put your FOCUS. To transform your attitude towards how and where you spend your time as a leader, you need to change the way you think about time and how you approach your tasks. It is impossible to squeeze everything into just one day. Rather, don't think and talk about time, opt for FOCUS instead! As one of the managing directors I interviewed said:

> "One of the keys to success is how well I can keep the focus."

Why is FOCUS important? Because you are a leader. Because your focus determines your organisation's focus and vice versa. Setting the right focus for your organisation starts with you, by setting your focus right. And by learning how to keep and adjust your focus without falling apart or losing your credibility. Therefore, you cannot forget about yourself in this matter. You as a leader should be in the middle of it. It is as much about the company, about the teams, about being successful and living a sustainable, fulfilling life as anything else. The former cannot be achieved without the latter.

Most leaders I interviewed find it challenging to determine and keep the right focus due to uncertainty, the increasing speed of today's business world, and information overload. Interestingly, only a couple of them found it not so difficult to determine the focus itself, but to find a good focus, because there are so many factors that need to be taken into consideration. The bigger and more complex the organisation the harder it is to keep their focus.

## Leadership insights

"It needs constant checking whether we are still heading in the right direction or if we should alter our focus; it is like shooting at a moving object."

"In the heavy mix of information and disinformation, it is a big challenge to decide what piece of information should I pick up. What is or should be on my radar and what system do I need to set up to prevent certain topics from falling off my radar screen? Finding the right technique and system of staying focused is crucial."

"It is so easy to be tempted and distracted on an opportunistic basis, because trying new ideas is more appreciated and applauded these days, but at the end of the day you as a leader have to set the flag somewhere."

"In 2017, our target was sharply set with a binocular rifle, but then it suddenly was blown up and we started acting in such haste, like shooting at mosquitoes with a shotgun. I felt at the beginning of 2020 that we were doing everything, and we were all over the place, but at the end of the day, the result was nothing. That's why focus is so important."

In my work with leaders and executives I approach leadership FOCUS and develop leaders in the following 5 areas:

- Functionality dimension of leadership FOCUS
- Pareto Principle (20/80) and leadership FOCUS

- A systemic approach to leadership FOCUS
- Flexibility in leadership FOCUS
- Managing self-limiting tendencies in leadership FOCUS

In this chapter, we will explore what these areas mean and how I work with leaders to master this leadership quality.

**Reflection points**

- Where is your focus right now?
- Where do you want to spotlight?
- What happens when you lose focus?
- What are the consequences, the positive and negative impacts of your losing focus?
- Where do you need to sharpen yourself to gain mastery in this leadership quality?

## The functionality dimension of leadership FOCUS

As we saw in the Introduction, you as a leader work in 3 domains when it comes to functionality: strategy, development, and operations. Self-awareness is key here. You need to make a conscious effort to see how you allocate your time and energy.

From the functionality dimension, you split your focus among the 3 domains (Figure 6.1).

**Figure 6.1: Functionality dimensions of leadership FOCUS (Source: Author's own).**

As a leader, you should spend most of your time in the strategic domain. That should be your number one priority in functioning as a leader. Let's say about 50% of your efforts should go there, with 30% on developmental activities, and only 20% on operations. Managers spend their time the other way around (operations first, development second, and strategy third). Of course, there are overlapping areas that can fall under both or all 3 areas depending on how you approach and tackle the task at hand. Let's cover what falls under each domain (Figure 6.2).

**Strategic domain:** Here we talk about tasks, events, and interactions that are more future-forward and long-term focused. They enhance the competitive advantage and effectiveness of your organisation, by looking into future trends, creating a vision and strategy for yourself and the organisation, taking risks to foster innovation and harness disruptions, providing directions and making big decisions, building both internal and external networks, creating alignments and re-alignments, and leveraging greater influence and impact through inspiration and empowerment. The problem with being overloaded

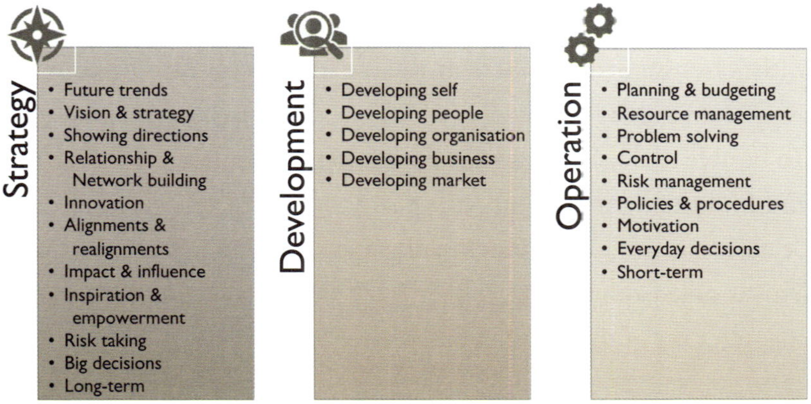


**Figure 6.2: Task allocation in the functionality dimension of Leadership FOCUS (Source: Author's own).**

and overscheduled is that you will never have the time for reflection; it is crucial to look at things from a distance, strategize, or generally perform the tasks in this sphere.

**Developmental domain**: In this domain, your main focus is on developing your people, your organisation, the business, and the market. But all these cannot be achieved authentically without developing yourself as a leader. This is the second most important area of leadership when it comes to functionality. Depending on the size and maturity of your company, and the mandate you signed up for, it could be as important as strategy.

**Operational domain:** All tasks, events, and interactions related to the operation of an organisation fall under this domain, such as planning and budgeting; managing resources; solving everyday, short-term and medium-term problems; introducing and monitoring control by policies and procedures; managing risks; motivating people on a daily basis; and making everyday decisions. I have noticed that many leaders tend to submerge themselves way too much in operational tasks and as a result, they create confusion for themselves by not knowing what their role as a leader should be. They often interfere unnecessarily with jobs assigned to others in the organisation. Learning to move away from the day-to-day operations is essential to becoming a leader. To be able to do that you need to develop and empower your people and find the right amount and quality of control to put in place to be able to carry out reality-checking and sampling to lead effectively. This is called zooming in, which I will talk about more later in this chapter. One of the leaders I interviewed noted:

> "My role is to provide direction and the related key indicators. To keep the direction is the role of the operational managers."

### Reflection exercise

Let's pause here and have a look at your calendar. How did you spend your time and energy in the last two weeks? Mark every item according to the 3 domains: S for strategic, D for developmental, and O for operational tasks, activities, or related events. This will give you an 'as is' status in the percentage of the functionality dimension of your current leadership focus.

If the 'as is' status shows that you spend way too much time on operational issues, which happens with a lot of leaders, you need to re-align your focus and redesign your forthcoming days and weeks.

Where do you have too much involvement as a leader? What is the reason behind this? Don't validate your reasons for too much involvement in one dimension; doing so means you are trying to find excuses for not doing the right things as a leader.

These reasons may be valid to a certain extent or for a short period. Perhaps you don't have the right person for the job; therefore, you need to get involved in the daily decision-making. Your role here is either to develop the best candidate in-house for the role or recruit the best one from the market. Sometimes you need to look behind the facade where the most obvious solutions lie. For example, the person next in line may be the solution. There is always hidden potential in your team. They only need to be recognised, empowered, and supported in their job and in their development by you as a leader. And, as a leader, that is your role.

Most interviewed leaders emphasised the importance of different elements of the strategic domain in their leadership roles. For example, seeing the big picture, creating the vision, and seeing the route ahead. Many also emphasised the importance of their role in the development domain by focusing on the growth of their people, organisation, and business.

## Leadership insights

"The light at the end of the tunnel does not change. The purpose (why we exist) and values of the organisation don't change. And if everything is built on these two, you can keep the focus."

"It is important to shape the vision, translate it into your own imagination and language, and to strongly believe in it. Otherwise, you can easily create a lot of discrepancies in the organisation."

"The real task is to find the strategy that helps you keep the focus. If you create a good strategy, which I created in 2017, you don't have to change anything. It helped us keep focus because it was and still is a good strategy. It doesn't mean we don't sniff around and search for 'new cheese' all the time."

"Here is the difference between leadership and management. As long as we are talking about management, the focus is very clear: you need to have clear goals with KPIs, educate people, deliver results, and do the work that is needed to achieve these. As far as leadership is concerned, it is like sailing at the sea, from here to there. On the ocean where winds blow from all directions and waves vary. That's hard but exciting at the same time."

"Leaders have to have a future focus and prepare the organisation for recognising and grabbing opportunities quickly. Even if we see the future trends but don't prepare, we can still make the relevant moves but the impact will be negative. Because 6 months later, we are still filling the holes created in the system. As an SME company, we don't have 6 months to build the muscles; we need to build them along the way and the leaders' role is to see what muscles we need to build, so we can be ahead of change, even if only a tiny bit."

"My role is to keep the focus on the continuous growth of the business, the organisation, and the people. Nothing more, nothing less."

"The right focus for the organisation is to strive to make people feel good. We set a focus that people feel connected to. They see what's in it for them, and what they can achieve here, and this is reflected in the results. Defining the focus is the responsibility of the leader. It cannot be passed on to people, although they should be involved in the crafting."

## Pareto Principle (20/80) and leadership FOCUS

The most comprehensive book written on the Pareto Principle is by Richard Koch titled *The 80/20 Principle: The Secret to Achieving More with Less*. I never imagined that the Pareto Principle could be used with such power in so many areas. Let's explore where this Pareto Principle comes from. The pattern underlying the 80/20 principle was discovered in 1897 by Italian economist Vilfredo Pareto (1848–1923). His discovery has since been called many names including the Pareto Principle, the Pareto Law, the 80/20 Rule, the 80/20 Principle, the Principle of Least Effect, and the Principle of Imbalance. He discovered that 80% of the land in Italy was owned by 20% of the population. After surveying several other countries, he found the same pattern abroad. For the most part, the Pareto Principle is an observation that things in life are distributed unevenly (Koch, 2014).

The Pareto Principle is based on pattern recognition. It can be applied in a wide range of areas in business, such as strategy, quality inventory management, project and resource management, and so on.

As Figure 6.3 shows there are two categories in the Pareto Principle (Koch, 2014):

- 80% – the majority that has little impact.
- 20% – the small minority that has a major impact.

There are two major types of applications:

- **Analysis** – which is about quantitative data. It is a systematic approach, a method of comparing cause/input and effect/output. It requires investigation and provides facts for leaders.
- **Thinking** – which is about qualitative data. It is a broader, less precise, and more intuitive procedure. It requires thought and provides insights for leaders.

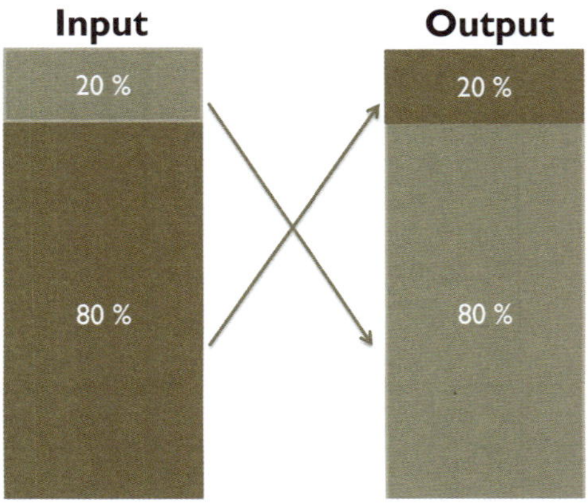


**Figure 6.3: The Pareto Principle - 80% of the outputs result from 20% of the inputs (Visual Paradigm Online, 2021).**

The Pareto Principle is also called the 80/20 Principle, but I prefer calling it the 20/80 Principle because you must put your focus on the 20%! This thinking capacity is strategic because it makes you concentrate on what is important. By using it you can decide what to do and what not to do. And sometimes deciding what not to do is the hardest. As a leader, you always have to see the vital few or find the highest value activities to focus on for both yourself and your organisation. Therefore, you must be selective and firm.

Maxwell (2018) and Koch (2014) make some interesting points:

- 20% of the products bring 80% of the profit.
- 80% of the profit comes from 20% of the client portfolio.
- 80% of the total sales revenue is generated by 20% of the salesforce.
- 20% of the results are achieved by 80% of the time invested.
- 80% of the results come from 20% of the effort.
- 80% of traffic jams happen on 20% of the roads.
- 80% of classroom activity is generated by 20% of the students.
- 20% of motorists cause 80% of road accidents.

- 80% of customer complaints are made about 20% of products and services.
- 20% of a system's faults cause 80% of its problems.

Focus on the 20% that brings you 80% results in respect of success, money, and enjoyment, not the other way around. My experience with leaders shows that it is easier to say this than to do it, of course.

Figuring out what the 20% is, is not easy. You must be precise, like a surgeon with a sharp scalpel. And because you may be afraid of what will happen with the remaining 80%. You have to weed it out, drop it, cut it out, or stop doing it because it has very little impact on the results, on the performance, and others (teams, organisation). Or if it is still necessary to keep any of the 80%, you should either delegate it, outsource it, or find the minimum viable solution. Or simply just use contractors for those tasks. The magic (and the hard work) lies in defining the minimum viable product. How can you narrow it down to a minimal scope that still delivers value to the customer? How can you simplify the process or pin down the minimum requirements or quality needed? What is the absolute minimum you can do and still deliver some value to your customer or any key stakeholders?

I don't use the analysis part of the Pareto Principle with my clients. Rather, I advocate the thinking capacity described, which is much broader and less precise and perhaps a more intuitive procedure. It is a non-quantitative application of the Pareto Principle. The 20/80 thinking is reflective, nonlinear, and unconventional. To make it happen you must slow down now in order to speed up later.

A day is 24 hours. Apparently, it is not enough for almost all leaders I interviewed, or for anyone. The Pareto Principle teaches you to see the wood from the trees, to concentrate on the most important tasks and exercise control of your life with the least possible effort. It's ideal for making targeted efforts instead of pursuing every available opportunity. To achieve that, you must be selective, because you cannot excel in many things. It will be hard because you'll have to say NO to many things.

It's not an easy choice. It requires awareness, discipline, continuous self-reflection, and asking yourself the same questions again and again. What I like about this approach is that it is very pragmatic. Be careful not to fall into the trap of numbers and figures in this respect. For example, if you have fewer sales of certain products or services with higher margins and more potential for add-on sales, it is still worth keeping them in your portfolio. You need to have your eyes open to look at the wider picture and make decisions with knowledgeable effort, time, and resources.

---

## Leadership insights

"We have to teach leaders to be able to identify focus, to keep focus, and to make their organisational unit focused. It requires not only constant work from them, but senior leadership needs to communicate the required message related to focus transparently and continuously. It entails a short and ongoing feedback loop to check whether the organisation has got that message (a limited number of key points to remember). If there are many organisational levels, the message can get distorted easily. Therefore, we, leaders, must communicate directly with different levels, and the 'why' should be included in that message."

"Re-focus, re-focus, get back onto the track when a detour is inevitable. I always perform 3 important tasks daily. 'What will be the results? Why are we here? Why are we doing it?' Asking these questions all the time is important for me to remain on track."

"It is getting harder and harder to keep the focus. The top 3 priorities are already difficult to set. The list always goes up to 5 and 6 and so on. Somehow you have to set the top 3. What makes it difficult is that the market is segmented, you have to pay attention to a lot: you have to deal with an increasingly complex world with impulses and disruptions from many directions and places."

"We are getting so many directions from global leadership, and they are sometimes contradictory, which means approximately 10 messages per day. What I use as a tool is to find the one that is very important, the rest I put aside. What is the one I should focus on!"

"Focus on 3 or maximum 5 things that are the strategic goals for the year. These should also be a maximum of 3 to 5 elements. Where there are 6 to 8 strategic goals, there is no strategic goal. There is no clear strategy, no clear focus."

---

With the help of the Pareto Principle, you could be more effective, more balanced, more profitable, and deliver a much more useful and impactful outcome. The key here is to learn how to distinguish the essential things from the non-essential ones.

If you want your life to be less complicated and more productive, you should focus your attention on the best 20% of what you do.

Maxwell (2015) changed from being "a doer of many things to a leader of few things". There's a lesson here for all leaders.

### Reflection points

- Ask yourself constantly: What is the 20% here that is leading me to the 80%?
- What is preventing you and your teams from focusing on the 20%?
- Who are the top 20% of your people you should focus on?
- Where and how can you use the Pareto Principle in your day-to-day activity, in your client portfolio, and in your leadership?
- If tomorrow's 20% (tasks, events, focus) will be different from today's 20%, where will they come from?

## A systemic approach to leadership FOCUS

Effective leaders have great pattern-recognition skills. In fact, one of the factors that distinguish a leader from a manager is how they approach problems. You probably became a manager because you stood out from your peers by being great at problem-solving and decision-making. Therefore, it is extremely hard for many leaders, including you, to let these strengths go. As a leader, it is not you who has to solve complex problems. Your task is to facilitate complex problem-solving in your organisation. Your people need to solve complex problems. Your role in this is to connect the dots, bring people together, and synergise. Or, and this is the important part, your role is to solve problems at a systemic level. To do that you need to recognise systemic issues and systemic patterns.

You need to distance yourself to see, recognise, assess, and respond to patterns at a systemic level instead of responding to particular cases. Don't look at the problems/issues in your organisation as separate, fragmented pieces. Your added value as a leader is to look at your organisation from a helicopter's vantage point.

At what level do you solve problems? You may find it hard to back off and too often you are too eager to jump in. This is the cradle of micro management. The culprit here is your ego. You were appointed as a leader because you are good at problem-solving and decision-making, but here you have to step back and let go of what you're really good at.

When you look closer at complexity, you see details and fragmented pieces. When you look at complexity from a distance you can see a series of simple and recurring patterns. The sources of systemic patterns are in many cases the management reports available for leaders, including you. Although not in all cases.

It's better to use a meta-view or a helicopter view in a more holistic way to see how the various components work together to deliver value. You can shift your perspective by using many lenses. Inviting people who hold totally different views into the conversation is valuable; build on this. Sometimes seeing things through the lens of opportunity gives you a totally different systemic perspective.

Eric C. Hanse and Ron A. Carucci (2014), in their book *Rising to Power,* identified 4 major types of systemic patterns for leaders (Figure 6.4) to recognise and deal with.

**Figure 6.4: Four major types of systemic patterns (Amended from source: Hanse and Carucci, 2014).**

### *Historical patterns*

Knowing and considering the history of an organisation (successes, failures, struggles, growth, reputation, etc.) is essential before making decisions to be able to predict how the organisation will respond and how well the organisation may perform in the future.

Stepping back and looking at patterns instead of isolated events helps you take the right actions and reach good decisions. It also helps you address upcoming issues along the way. It doesn't mean you are using the past as an excuse like "We tried to implement this before, but it didn't work. I think it doesn't work in this environment" or "We tried acquisitions before, but the integration derailed; therefore, we shouldn't do it" or "We got burnt once; we shouldn't go into that direction again." It does mean using the past as a reference point for choices about future changes. Learn from the experience and incorporate the learning into future decisions. This is how you can use these patterns.

## *Horizontal patterns*

Patterns across the organisation reveal emerging norms that may or may not be desirable. Unfortunately, many leaders tend to pick up on informal and rather unreliable comments in line with their own preconceptions as a generalisation. For example, 'Everybody is feeling frustrated because....' or 'I've heard from all over the organisation that...'. Instead of digging in, assessing, and really understanding what these true patterns are and where they're coming from, leaders often make assumptions and rather frail attempts to identify these patterns across the organisation. They feel that these patterns are messy and take too much time to unfold. For example, the misuse of insufficient and unreliable data across the company may not only be about the lack of capabilities but also about people being afraid of losing their jobs due to difficult market conditions. The inadequate response from leadership can put even more pressure on the system to perform even better, which will result in less useful and less accurate data, as more people feel compelled to make things up. It can also generate distrust and unhealthy competition within an organisation. For example, in an area where sales are not the strongest, the competence of the specialised middle-managers might be questioned; putting pressure on them to achieve certain targets may lead them to make up fictional events and tasks and distort reality to protect themselves in front of their leadership.

### *Economic patterns*

Economic patterns come from looking across a range of data sets, for example, megatrends, sales trends, industry trends, geographic buying patterns, margins, costs, cash reserves, and so on to see what important message emerges from this data. The challenges for leaders are twofold here. First, many organisations still lack the analytical capability to spot early economic shifts, both in their marketplaces as well as in their organisations. Secondly, many leaders operate with a short-term focus and spend way too much time in the operational instead of the strategic domain.

As a leader, make it a daily habit to monitor the market locally, regionally, and globally and the geopolitical movements across the world. This is your ongoing homework.

### *Cultural patterns*

There are tons of surveys available today; for example, employee engagement surveys, organisational health surveys, online employee feedback tools, as well as communication channels such as newsletters, town hall meetings, and intranet sites. Still, the small degree to which collected data is leveraged to increase the overall health of the organisation, or the engagement of employees, is striking. Many leaders approach these surveys as a kind of tick-the-box exercise, delegate them to HR, and take the easiest action steps. However, truly understanding the insights into cultural patterns enables leaders to make strategic choices about how to shape and shift the organisation's behaviour to ensure that employees from top to bottom are fully participating in optimising performance. Remember: "Culture is a tidal wave. You don't stand a chance" (Gapingvoid, 2019).

According to my work with executives and leaders and based on the interview data collected, this is the least developed area in leadership

FOCUS. Leaders rarely recognise systemic patterns, let alone deal with them and when they do, they do it unconsciously. So, developing pattern recognition skills along with a systemic approach to organisational issues is a huge area for development for leaders.

### Reflection points

- What patterns can you recognise in the history of your organisation before you embark on a new change?
- What cultural patterns emerge if you look at the last 4 employee engagement surveys of your organisation?
- Through systemic lenses what patterns can you detect in the information you are receiving?
- Where do your teams work seamlessly across the organisation?
- Where do you see tensions and detachments that undermine performance?

## Flexibility in FOCUS

How can you be focused and flexible at the same time? In today's business environment both are essential to success. Imagine a scale or a range on which there are two sometimes opposing but valid stands. You as a leader have to be able to switch between broad and narrow perspectives, between long- and short-term thinking, between past and future, and so on. Sometimes it's not about moving up and down on the scale, but rather it is about finding the right balance between the two in any given situation.

Interviewed leaders not only see the need and the place for more flexibility when it comes to focusing, but they also refer to their so-called gut feeling, which is the grey area in their decision-making process.

### *Zooming in vs zooming out*

Crafted leaders can zoom in and zoom out. They can look at the big picture and understand the details. Leaders should spend more time in zoom-out mode by looking at the whole context, at the organisation as a system that is part of a larger ecosystem, and understanding the changing landscape. Their main role is to ask questions, make observations, and challenge the organisation from that distanced vantage point.

Nevertheless, they cannot lose contact with the reality, the here and now of their organisation, which happens at the day-to-day operations level. Therefore, they need to learn to dive in to get samples, ask thought-provoking and controlling questions, challenge the norm and status quo, and fly back high into helicopter view.

When leaders dive in, and spend more time with the details and pixels of the whole picture, they may end up micro-managing. It is essential to design how to dive in, and what kind of controlling system is needed to be able to stay relevant and understand what is happening on the floor. Also, leaders need to make sure that they change their way of controlling from time to time, as people get used to providing the same answers and data requested, and at some point, the data starts to get distorted. One fundamental human factor kicks in here: everyone wants to show their best work, their best face to their leader, and hide the ugly side from them. Most of the time people do this with good intentions, without ill will. So, leaders start seeing things from a narrow perspective with positive cosmetics.

If, as a leader, you learn how to change your controlling checkpoints from time to time and make sure that you dig deeper here and there, you will be able to get the right quality and number of samples from your organisation without spending too much time in zoom-in mode. This requires not only conscious effort but also a lot of energy.

### *Short-term vs long-term*

This is a classic challenge in leadership. The only difference now is that the pressure is more acute from both directions. Today's leaders need to deliver results no matter what and at the same time, they need to prepare their organisation for the future. Finding the right balance is a challenge for every leader, i.e., how they can make both ends meet. The COVID-19 pandemic increased the importance of short-termism. The long-term has been shortened these days. We are no longer talking about 5-year strategies, of 2 or a maximum of 3 years. However, leaders need to consider what Paul Polman from Unilever rightly said: "Too many CEOs play the quarterly game and manage their business accordingly. But many of the world's challenges cannot be addressed with a quarterly mindset" (Morgan, 2020). Short-termism is also negatively correlated with innovativeness, which has become one of the key competitive advantages of any organisation.

Flexibly moving from here and now to where the organisation is heading and not losing the focus on the long-term is your role as the leader. You have the compass in your hands; make sure to use it. When you spend too much time in operational mode, you lose focus of the long term and neglect the compass.

### *Past vs future*

Just because something worked in the past does not mean it will work in the present or the future. In fact, today's rapidly changing environment guarantees that whatever leadership technique you apply, the context will be always different and continuously, fluidly changing. This is the very reason you cannot use past recipes in leadership. One of the interviewed leaders nailed it:

> "Focus is a current state, but I need to know the focus for the future. For me, as a leader, the important thing is what the focus will be, and where to pay attention. It is my job as a leader to pay attention to these, and to follow them."

Also, a significant shift occurring in leadership is that planning based on past financial results and benchmarks from past patterns is no longer helping the organisation to get ahead of the game in their industry.

Build future into your planning process, setting key results indicators based less on past results than on the future potential of the current or the future organisation. Work hard to predict, envision, and prepare yourself and your organisation for something that is not yet here.

---

### Leadership insights

"When the leader's focus is on solving today's problems in the present, not looking ahead, they are not living the future, and they are surely out of focus. The leader who lives today is definitely out of focus. The leader who solves today's problems is already at fault. Today's problems must be solved by their team. The leader's task is to ensure that the problems of today will never occur again and prepare themselves and their organisation for what will be the future problems."

"Everything is constantly changing. The world is complex. Many times, we only know or rather feel where we are going and how to get to the final destination, how much flexibility there is on the road. The final destination is fixed, but we must not become blind, because everything may move on and change."

"Flexibility is needed, and constant iterative thinking about what I look at, at what level I need to look at things and what is needed for me to follow up. It's hard. And I rely quite a lot on my gut feelings and intuition as well."

"Zoom out and zoom in, one does not exist without one or the other. But it is very tiring to switch suddenly and retune. Sometimes I lose my reality. I have to give complex answers to complex problems, and when I do that, I have to remind myself to step back a bit, ask myself what our goal is and, in the end, this always gives me the answer. So, zooming in and zooming out is important."

"Zooming out for me is spending 3 days in the office. It is all about the main goal, which I think about all year round. Like all top executives, I have the same annual KPIs, EBT, EBIDA, sales targets. Zooming in for me is spending 2 days in the field to see what is really happening and visiting franchise stores to ask questions and collect answers."

"Zoom in or zoom out, both are required. If you don't have the zoom out you are not a leader. If you don't have the zoom in, it can still work but you can lose reality and it very much depends on the organisation. Zooming in for a long time means micromanaging for me."

"I focus more on the zoom out than on zoom in now. When I was appointed to Managing Director from a Finance Director position, at the beginning I had too much of a financial lens. I saw and approached everything through numbers. Luckily, I trusted the new Finance Director, so I gradually let it go. But I had to learn it and it took time. This can be a trap for many leaders."

---

### Reflection points

- How can you master flexibility in your leadership FOCUS?
- Learn what your natural tendencies are. Where do you feel more comfortable (in zoom-in or zoom-out mode, short-term activities or long-term activities, to build on the past or build on the future)? What are the consequences of neglecting the other end of each range?
- Be aware of how much energy is required from you in moving across these ranges. Where do you leak the most energy?
- What conscious effort or personal system do you need to put in place to be able to keep your focus and at the same time be flexible?
- What controlling questions do you need to ask? When and where do you need to change your controlling questions as data may get distorted?

## Managing self-limiting tendencies in leadership FOCUS

### *Fish in the bowl*

You may have heard the adage "The fish is the last to discover water." It means it can be difficult to see, to be aware of something when you are so absorbed in it. Living and breathing in the same bubble can easily blindside a leader. We all have blind spots. But what happens when a leader has blind spots? It matters even more as many people are affected by their decisions and their actions.

One of the typical leadership blind spots that I've often encountered during my work with executives is that in an overly familiar working environment they do not see their impact on others. Leaders tend to assume that all of their followers have the same motivations, values, communication and behavioural styles as they do. They tend to hire 'mini me' leadership team members because they can easily connect with them. They don't recognise when they have a negative impact, when they're accidentally insensitive to cultural and behavioural differences, criticising and devaluing others for the sake of improvement with good intentions. And all these happen because of familiarity and making too many assumptions.

Stepping back, challenging your own status quo, questioning basic routines or just simply bringing someone in who asks the difficult questions helps a lot to see more of the reality of the whole and expand your own perception.

There's a saying in Hungarian that new managing directors use a lot: *Esnek ki a csontvázak a szekrényből – skeletons fall out of the closet.* The skeletons are old ways of doing things, old habits, tasks, processes, shortcuts, unfinished business, and debris swept under the carpet. Eventually, leaders not only easily get used to them but become so attached to them that there is very little chance that they will recognise and deal with them.

It's easier to notice skeletons when you take up a new managing director position because when you look for them, you have a fresh eye to spot them. But when you have been with the organisation for a long time you won't notice them. You need to train your eyes and set your focus to search for them. Asking yourself and others basic, sometimes too obvious questions, is a good tool. Why do you do what you do and why do you do it in the way you do it? Look for the shortcuts. Sometimes identifying what needs to be changed in your organisation is rather difficult because you have become so accustomed to the problem you can no longer see it clearly.

How can you obtain fresh perspectives and how can you have fresh eyes?

Watching your company movie, distancing yourself, being in a zoom-out mode or getting into an imaginary helicopter can help you see your company from a distance. A fresh eye can also reveal a lot about your company.

The tricky things about blind spots and skeletons are that you as well as your people have learnt to live with them, to avoid them, to work around them. Only very few people have the courage to confront them in order to bring them to the surface and address them.

### Reflection points

- What are you not seeing, not noticing?
- What are you missing? What do you need?
- Whose perception/lens do you need to borrow?
- How can you uncover your leadership blind spots? Who can help you with that?
- What are your organisation's blind spots?
- When and to what extent do people seek you out, avoid you, or work around you?

#### *Setting and keeping boundaries*

Setting and keeping your boundaries for the sake of yourself and for the sake of your organisation is not easy. But to be focused you must make targeted efforts to succeed and that requires saying NO to many things. The second reason to set boundaries is to protect yourself as a human being. Yes, you as a leader also have physical limitations.

To what or to whom do you need to say NO? Do you find it hard...

- **saying NO to others?** Most of the time leaders, including you, have no problems saying no to others. But on rare occasions when you are too good a corporate citizen or due to lack of confidence you say yes to your own leaders or your shareholders or to key stakeholders because you may be afraid of damaging the relationship by saying no. Nevertheless, what you do is sign up for something you don't truly believe in. As a result, you are partly committed; you demonstrate half-heartedness and send mixed messages to your people, which creates confusion.

- **saying NO to things?** I have heard many times "When I reach the next promotion, when I finish this huge international project, when I complete this organisational transformation, everything will be much easier. I will slow down a bit." What actually happens is that you compromise. You trade off your family time, your health, your friends, your energy till you realise you have burnt out, you have lost your passion and, in fact, you've lost yourself on the way.
- **saying NO to your internal driving force?** Many leaders, including you, have a great ambition to build the organisation and grow the business. That's why you are a leader. You have strong entrepreneurship. The risk here is to take up too many things. You may tend to overburden your organisation and if you forget about the celebration of achievements and successes, people will become frustrated, feel undervalued, get burnt out, and then leave. People and teams need to have recovery phases before they jump onto the next big thing. One leader I spoke to asked:

  "How much is enough? My own leadership focus is on constant growth. This is my driving force as well. I guess I have a personal deficiency; for me nothing is enough. Satisfaction is not there, but it does not bother me because it has a positive strong effect on results, and on our performance."

  How can you control yourself and say NO to your constant desire to take on more and more? The other area where you can find it challenging to say no to your inner driving force is when you are a banyan tree; if you are this type of leader, you protect and shield your people, but nothing grows under you. Most of the time you do this with good intentions; however, the impact is quite diminishing for both the teams and the organisation.

It might seem that you distrust the judgement and capabilities of others. If you are a "saviour" or a "mother hen" type of leader, you condition your people to be dependent which decreases ownership, proactiveness, and initiative-taking within your organisation. So, you have to turn down this force in you and let your people develop through failure; don't do the difficult jobs for and instead of them.

- **saying NO to your inclination to have a finger in every pie?** Get out of the way when you as a leader become a barrier in your organisation. Sometimes when you are too much in the present, you are way too much into the operational side. This is a control and trust issue.
- **saying NO to the 24-hour open-door policy?** Today's trends for modern leadership and organisation are about being absolutely accessible and sitting with people in an open office. This sounds fantastic, but if you implement it, you are no longer able to focus. You end up being interrupted all the time. You put the control of your focus into the hands of the environment. In addition to that, we are well equipped with modern technologies where there are many interferences (digital sounds) and disruptions (news alerts, email notifications, pop-ups) that create a continuous distraction in our days.

So how do you conquer the boundary issues? Create your own personal systems with rules in addition to mastering the art of letting go. To sharpen your FOCUS, you must give up guilt related to excessive and endless hard work and the desire to attend to everything; otherwise, you become a leader no one wants to follow, especially younger generations.

### Reflection points

- Where do you neglect your boundaries? Where do you let others take advantage of you?
- Where do you find it difficult to say NO?
- To whom do you find it difficult to say NO?
- What do you find it difficult to say NO to?
- What systems and rules do you need to be able to say NO more in all these areas?

### *The trap of multitasking*

Leaders spend their entire days with a bunch of overlapping simultaneous tasks. I have seen calendars that were not only fully booked but with double or triple clashes of appointments. Multitasking means trying to perform two or more tasks simultaneously.

Research conducted at Stanford University found that multitasking is less productive than doing a single thing at a time (Gorlick and Hubbard, 2009). We are more prone to errors and mistakes while we are multitasking. Researchers also found that people who are regularly bombarded with several streams of electronic information cannot pay attention, recall information, or switch from one job to another as well as those who complete one task at a time (Bradberry, 2014).

In this fast-paced world, multitasking may seem like the most efficient way to get everything done. However, the truth is that multitasking reduces your efficiency and performance because your brain can only focus on one thing at a time.

Studies also show that when our brains are constantly switching back and forth between tasks, especially when we deal with complex issues, we become less efficient and more likely to make a mistake. Dave Crenshaw in his book *The Myth of Multitasking* says there is no such thing as multitasking, only switchtasking, i.e., repeatedly switching back and forth between tasks. It is costly, inefficient, and ineffective. So, we fool ourselves. It is less apparent when we do it with routine, single tasks, but still, we do it.

Kim Clark and Steven Wheelwright (1993) studied the effects of multitasking and found that the time we spend on value-adding work drops rapidly when we are working on more than two tasks. With one assigned task, individuals were able to spend approximately 70% of each day on that task. In most companies the remaining 30% went to answering emails, attending meetings, having impromptu conversations with colleagues (about work or not), and so on. According to the study, things look even better when participants were given a second task. In that case, they were able to spend 80% of their time on those two tasks. If multitasking across 2 tasks is good, then 3, 4, or 5 tasks must be even better, right? Clark and Wheelwright (1993) found the opposite: When working on 3 tasks, the total time on tasks dropped to 60%, an average of 20% on each of the 3 tasks.

Also, one of the characteristics of being in a flow state (i.e., in the zone, fully immersed in a feeling of energised focus,) is complete concentration on a task. You cannot achieve flow by multitasking throughout your life.

According to Crenshaw (2021), there are two types of switches:

- **Active switches:** Switching tasks to make a call, flip through your mail, talk to someone. Any time you make a switch it is an active switch.
- **Passive switches:** Someone or something other than you makes the switch. For example, you get a text message notification, or someone interrupts you.

The higher you are on the hierarchy, the more responsibility you have, and the more you experience passive switches.

Crenshaw (2021) also talks about backtasking. While multitasking is inefficient, backtasking can be both efficient and effective. Backtasking is when you are eating dinner while watching a webinar or running while listening to podcasts. The reason why this works is that only one task requires your attention; the other one does not need it at all.

Many of you think you can attend to many things at the same time, but actually what is happening is that you divide your attention among many things and don't pay full attention to any one of them. And if you're not paying full attention to one thing, or indeed anything, you cannot excel.

There is a Hungarian saying: *Aki sokat markol, keveset fog – who grabs a lot takes a little.* How much do you grab?

**What can you do to avoid the trap of multitasking?**

- Choose to tackle one task at a time. Remember to choose the 20% that brings you the 80% result.
- Set up recurring meetings with people who regularly want to ask questions, report to you, consult with you, share information

with you, etc. The more frequent the meeting is, the shorter it should be. No more than 15 minutes. The less frequent the meeting is, perhaps monthly, the longer it should take, for example, 60 minutes.

- Set up an outgoing voicemail saying when you will return calls. Give 2 one-hour time ranges per day.
- Set up open-door periods when you are fully available for anyone in the office.
- Limit digital interruptions. Silence your notification alerts. You control your phone, not the other way around.
- Block out time for the 20% before each week starts.
- Don't overschedule yourself. Only book 75% of your time. The rest is for any urgent matter or crisis.
- When you plan your week, remember the 7 hours of lost time (1 hour per day) due to accumulated small insignificant random everyday activities like standing up from your chair, opening the window, getting a snack, scratching your nose, etc. (Crenshaw, 2021).

Leaders live and work under enormous pressure because they have so much on their plates. They face so many disruptions and distractions. Most of them see technological advancement and devices as an opportunity for future growth and they hardly recognise the negative impact they have on their productivity and focus. They only feel that their day and attention are very much fragmented and by the end of the week, they feel exhausted. "Remember, the majority of what happens in business aren't really emergencies, they are impatiences" (Crenshaw, 2021).

## Leadership insights

"We should really use our common sense like the old people. My grandfather was a self-sufficient farmer. I helped him a lot in the fields when I was a boy. He had lots of work, but he never hurried. He was able to pay attention to many tasks, but never rushed. We finished one task and then moved to the next one. And there was a natural recovery session built into the annual cycle due to the nature of work. Today, companies keep moving to other new things before having the first-launched ones finished. And we are so afraid of being left behind, left out of anything. No wonder many of us burn out. Multitasking is the most inefficient existing thing on the planet."

"It is really difficult, because we've got lots of opportunities (fraud, new directions related to fraud ethics, compliance solutions, third party risk management and so on), and I am a bit greedy. I really enjoy them but find it difficult to say no to any of them."

"Sometimes I'm not there, I'm not present. I do 4 things in parallel all the time, but sometimes I don't know how I've got from A to B. This is scary as hell."

"It is terribly difficult in sales. We have 15 KPIs. One focus, two focuses, no focus. Really, I can't give them more than 2 things to focus on!"

A successful leader is focused! A successful business is a focused one!

# CHAPTER VI

# T is for TRUST

"Trust is the highest form of human motivation.
It brings out the very best in people."

(Covey, 2004)

## What is happening with TRUST today?

Unfortunately, trust, in general, is on the decline in our global society. Due to the unprecedented disaster of the COVID-19 pandemic and the turbulence of the economic crisis resulting from it, the 2021 Edelman Trust Barometer reports "an epidemic of misinformation and widespread mistrust of societal institutions and leaders around the world. Adding to this is a failing trust ecosystem unable to confront the rampant infodemic, leaving the 4 institutions – business, government, NGOs and media – in an environment of information bankruptcy and a mandate to rebuild trust and chart a new path forward" (Edelman, 2021).

Technological advancements have opened up our world, and made us feel that our planet was rather small. Despite full transparency, what is blurred with fogginess due to ambiguity and intentional or unintentional manipulations from all actors who are laying out many interpretations of any event. As a result of the COVID-19 pandemic, people lost their jobs in numbers equivalent to the Great Depression (Edelman, 2021). There is also a pervasive fear of job loss due to automation. This can also be seen as a great advancement but one which serves only the interests of a very limited number of people, for example, shareholders.

As we live in a very transparent world, integrity is more important than ever. It is not just about complying with the rules but also doing the right thing. Everything can become visible very quickly. Seeing right and wrong, which is more of a black-and-white perspective in the complexity of today, is not at all easy; in some cases, it's almost impossible.

It's not only the complexity of our business environment that makes trust a complex issue but also the speed of change and the requirements of responding quickly to market needs. These impact trust and make it even harder to see it as a stable force and foundation of any business.

Our world is also polarised to an extreme measure nowadays. Institutional trust is in greater jeopardy now than ever before. Many people feel let down and left behind. In the past, it was much easier to hide the wrongdoings of any leader. Trustworthiness is not newsworthy. Many media actors serve this polarised political agenda by distorting and exaggerating stories of actual events and showing them from a narrow and sometimes a single point of view.

Trust and influence now lie more with individuals than with institutions. This is the biggest trust shift in history. After the financial crisis in 2008, Brexit made visible the first wave of acute symptoms emerging from this shift. Signs of distributed trust are appearing.

Network organisations like social media, with their anonymity and lack of accountability, create this new phenomenon called distributed trust. The lack of quality information is because any information can be distributed by many faceless and unidentifiable people and groups. The internet has made it harder to differentiate facts from fiction and made it easier to undermine the truth (Botsman, 2017).

"Unfortunately, according to a study by Deloitte, less than half of millennials actually believe that businesses behave ethically and less than half believe that business leaders are working toward improving society as a whole" (Morgan, 2020:67).

The facets of trust are many how companies treat their people, what kind of ethical business practices they have, what is at stake if they do not act on data protection and cybersecurity, how they are addressing income inequality, how they can responsibly implement robotics and artificial intelligence with the right accountability, whether they have a fair balance between valuing profit and people, whether they are authentic and congruent in their communication both internally and externally, and so on.

The landscape of TRUST is complex, and I'm afraid it doesn't look so promising. Nevertheless, it must be the number one priority of leadership, because every business is a people business. And when there is no trust, things get complicated, success is not guaranteed, and companies can quickly lose their greatest assets: their people.

## The importance of TRUST

Trust is the glue that keeps our lives together, the fuel that motivates great teams, the cement in relationships. Unfortunately, it can be eroded little by little, day by day; on the other hand, it is also extremely fragile. One mistake, a wrongly worded, inappropriate sentence can ruin many years of hard work. It is difficult to recover trust, but not impossible.

Trust is one of the most important issues on the agenda of top leaders. It impacts the company's brand and reputation enormously and thus the financial performance of the company as well. People want to be sure that the leader they follow and work for is worthy of their trust. People simply don't trust leaders who can't live by their set of values, ethics, and standards. That is why it is so important to sharpen the REAL LEADER in you (Chapter I). CRAFTing the future and having a greater influence on wider society cannot be achieved without trust. Sustainable companies aim at a triple-bottom-line (profit, people, planet) instead of a single bottom-line, profit only. The importance of trust is greater when the market has matured and become saturated because this is the phase where the value of relationships comes to the fore. A leap in trust creates new possibilities. In today's world leaders need to break down barriers and form new relationships and partnerships that were not thought possible before.

Tackling the challenges and confronting the threats we face in the world cannot be done alone, at least not very effectively. It requires the help and support of others. So, people first should be the only way forward for any business as the others (profit and planet) cannot be achieved, addressed, and taken care of without people. "Trust is fundamental to almost every action, relationship and transaction" (Botsman, 2017:10). Therefore, trust must be reciprocal because it takes two to dance the tango. Or as John C. Maxwell puts it: "Trust is the heart of any relationship. Getting to know your people, build solid, lasting relationships, gain people's permission to lead" (Maxwell, 2013). The point here is to gain people's permission to lead, and you can only achieve this if they trust you to lead them.

We all want to be trusted, to belong to, to feel like we are welcome and a valuable part of a group. The leader's role is to create a "circle of safety" because that sense of belonging is a biological need of any human being. "Trust is a very special human experience produced by the chemical oxytocin" (Sinek, 2014:74).

Not only does it take time to build trust, but you also have to see the impact of your leadership in terms of trust. For example, when you zoom in to check your organisation and happen to stay there for too long, you start micro-managing your teams or acting like a glue between divisions. In such cases, you actually don't trust your people, or you show distrust unintentionally and it creates diminishing tendencies within your organisation.

"The only way you get trustworthiness into an organisation's blood is if the top leaders have it in their blood" (Blakley, 2016:3). Trustworthiness is a skill that can be developed.

Trust is subjective, contextual, circumstantial, and fragile. There must be a distinction between trust and trustworthiness. You can choose to be trustworthy; you can work on it but only others can decide whether they trust you. As Blakey puts it: "Your goal is to become worthy of the trust of others" (Blakey, 2016).

You must earn trust. You have to work hard to gain the trust of others. You have to prove yourself trustworthy. It starts with leadership. It starts with you!

According to Stephen M.R. Covey, author of *The Speed of Trust*, trust produces speed because it feeds collaboration, loyalty, and ultimately results. So, trust is very much needed in today's fast-moving, agile business environment (Covey, 2006).

It is also you, the leader, who decides what kind of environment you want to build. Trust is the basis of the culture for collaboration and sharing, which results in creativity, innovation, learning, and sharing not only successes but also failures.

I use the trust equation formula as a framework to generate discussion on trust with leaders. There are 4 primary components/variables to trustworthiness in the equation. In my work, I unfold how to develop trust in the following subsections:

- TRUST in self/TRUST self
- TRUST others (one-to-one, one-to-many: teams)
- The TRUST equation
- TRUST in economic terms
- TRUST in emotional terms
- TRUST others (one-to-many: organisations, networks)
- TRUST in the unknown
- The extra ingredient: TRUST in gratitude

## What makes a trustworthy leader according to the leaders I interviewed?

The common themes that emerged from the leadership interviews are that trustworthy leaders are credible leaders. They have high integrity. People can count on them. They are consistent and congruent. What they say and what they do are in line, and they follow up on their promises either by keeping them or if they cannot keep them, they go back to their people and explain why. If leaders keep promising and not delivering on their promises, sooner or later they will lose the trust of their people, even if they explain the reasons. So, the number one rule is: never make a promise you cannot keep. The interviewed leaders approach credibility from two aspects: 1) being a credible leader and 2) being credible and honest in their communication. They said that trustworthy leaders need to be accessible. They must be visible and have a strong leadership presence. Nothing generates trust more than when a leader tells the truth and speaks openly, especially about their own mistakes. They should not be afraid of showing their vulnerability. Almost all of the interviewed leaders mentioned the importance of empathy and transparency in trust. Trustworthy leaders can connect to their people outside the official agenda on a human-to-human level as trust is reciprocal. Trustworthy leaders have strong values and principles. They believe in those values and principles, rely on them, and live by them. Whatever a leader expects from their people in terms of behaviour, they must role-model first. Because everything starts with leadership. Trust starts with leadership.

---

## Leadership insight

"Trustworthiness means for me when my colleagues experience difficulties in their life, they have the courage to come up to me even with their personal problems, and I help them with these personal problems as much as possible. For example, someone's dad didn't have firewood for the winter, and we got it for him. Someone's child couldn't study at home during the lockdown of COVID-19 because his computer was broken, so we sent one to him. It requires a high level of trust from your people to share personal difficulties with their boss, which is sometimes embarrassing for them. From my side, it is important for me to help them as much as I can; that is the way we have such a loyal and supportive culture here. I believe a leader should not only be a good leader but a good person as well."

"If you have a handshake of a diamond dealer you are a trustworthy leader."

"Little everyday things matter in building trust. For example, thank the other person. Incorporate regular recognition of efforts and contributions, not only of results. Listen to what they have to say. Be interested in them as a person. Always own your part of the problem, task and say it out loud."

---

## TRUST in self/TRUST self

Self-confidence is partly about self-esteem and partly about a feeling of trust in your own abilities, which means that you trust yourself, your capabilities, and your current and future potential. The turbulence and unknown factors of today's business environment make you question your abilities from time to time and as a result, your self-confidence may erode.

No matter what your heritage is, for example, if you come from a Central and Eastern European country or another developing culture (and you are a woman) and end up in a regional or a global director role, you must dare to live up to the role internally as well. Don't be afraid that others will see you as weak due to your heritage and origin. Don't be apologetic. You have to put yourself onto a higher shelf internally first and foremost. You must be clear about what it takes to achieve that. This is very much of a mental and emotional shift.

Trust in self also means trusting your intuition. Let your gut feeling be part of your decision-making process, not only when you decide on a task but also on people.

Another dimension of trusting yourself is to trust your native genius. I have seen leaders who tend to lose it along the way of their leadership journey. Trusting yourself, your capabilities, your strengths, and your potential is really tested when you happen to be out of a job or in-between jobs or when you find yourself without a position and a title. Remember, leaders who trust in themselves and are resourceful survive even under the most challenging circumstances. They never cling to a position so desperately as if the position has become their identity.

Trust in self cannot be done without being clear about your values and honouring them, making continuous and intentional efforts to live by them.

Based on your preferences, cultural upbringing, and how you are wired, you can tap into your natural source of trust differently. Trust from the head is a cognitive-based trust, used widely in business. It is when you build trust by influencing others through rationale and logic. Trust from the heart is affect-based trust, when you build trust by influencing others through emotions; it is easier to tap into this trust with friends and family. And trust from the gut is instinct-based trust, which we tend to neglect or sometimes override with rationale and reasoning, especially in business (Botsman, 2017).

Trust in self also means you are confident enough to open yourself up to being vulnerable, to admit that you have made a mistake.

Building trust needs time. It requires investment, effort, and energy; therefore, efficiency and speed can be the enemy of trust. But before we move on to how to build trust with others first you must master the trust in self. Chapter I: Sharpen the REAL LEADER in you deals with this extensively, as you need to be clear about who you are, the REAL LEADER in you, and you must also be fully aware of your natural tendencies and preferences through profiling. The third element here is your self-limiting thoughts (your inner critic).

I was brought up in Central and Eastern Europe (in the communist era), and I have seen this lack of confidence due to self-limiting thoughts in clients who come from a less developed part of the world and a far too complying culture. We all need to overcome the barriers of our cultural heritage especially when we are invited to the table of the board of global directors.

### Reflection points

- What is your natural trust source (head, heart, or gut)?
- How much do you let your heart and gut influence your leadership style?
- How often do you listen to your intuition when you make a business or a people-related decision?
- When was the last time you admitted in front of others that you had made a mistake? What was your key learning about yourself? Have you shared your key learning?

Inner critic checking:

- What does the little voice in your head (your inner critic) keep telling you about yourself? What is it saying?

- Where are these views coming from and why?
- How is it affecting your day-to-day work, your relationships, and your performance?
- How can you turn down your inner critic's voice?

## TRUST others – one to one and one-to-many: teams

When it comes to trusting others, there are two aspects: 1) one-to-one trust and 2) one-to-many trust (team, organisation, partnership, networking).

We cannot go a day without exhibiting and experiencing trust at various levels. We all depend on trust in so many of our daily activities. The purpose of high-level trust is to develop a quality relationship with another person. This varies from situation to situation, from relationship to relationship, because trust is highly contextual and relational.

It takes two to build trust in a relationship because trust is a two-way street. If either party fails, quits, or avoids the other, trust disappears. It is also risky. But one thing is certain, leaders must be the first ones to make a move.

One-to-one trust means confidently relying on another person and getting to know the other person. "I know you would be there for me. We not only help each other but we are not afraid of holding each other accountable." It is a unique dance between two individuals. In a trusted relationship, we not only have expectations but tend to be more vulnerable.

Of course, again there are differences in terms of behavioural tendencies as well. Some leaders easily trust others genuinely and instinctively and there are leaders with whom trust has to be earned. One thing is certain: no one should take trust for granted in any of their relationships. Results- and task-focused leaders need to pay more attention to building trusted relationships with others as well. They naturally and only connect to people at the task level and not at a human level. But to build trusted relationships leaders cannot avoid or skip the latter.

Although some people need time to trust another, there are other people who genuinely and instinctively trust people, sometimes to the extent of naivety. In the case of transferred trust, this happens much faster. Transferred trust is when the new person is recommended by someone trusted by you so you give them the benefit of the doubt and trust them.

When building a high-performing team, you must pay attention to the level of trust within the team and how to build and facilitate a higher level of trust. "Trust is the glue that holds people together" (Maxwell, 2013:119). How can you create that glue in your team? According to Patrick Lencioni (2005), the absence of trust is the first dysfunction of a team to become a high performing effective team. Virtual teams work harder to develop high levels of trust. Trust is also fundamental to creating a sense of belonging in a team.

When facilitating trust within your team and organisation, you act as a facilitator by herding everyone in the direction of finding common ground; bridging the gap when there are great differences; connecting the dots; showing what makes a team strong; and showing how they can respect, honour, and appreciate each other's differences. It means committing, balancing, and openly and passionately involving everyone in the team in discussions and productive disagreements to move forward. You should also facilitate and role-model how you as a team are going to take responsibility for each other's weaknesses and hold each other accountable. Accountability is part of high-level trust; poor performance must have consequences and the same standard should apply to everyone. When you make strong and steady relationships, you accept 100% accountability in all matters. You should not be measuring, waiting for others to make a move, or blaming others for the problems and negative situations. Lencioni (2005) separates these two dysfunctionalities (lack of trust and lack of accountability), but I see them as a sister and a brother. I see accountability as a part of trust with respect to expectations of corporate standards, self, and others.

Although there are many great books and models/frameworks about trust, when I work with leaders and executives on trust, I really like using the Trust Equation formula introduced by Maister, Green, and Galford (2002) in the Trusted Advisor (Figure 7.1).

## The Trust equation

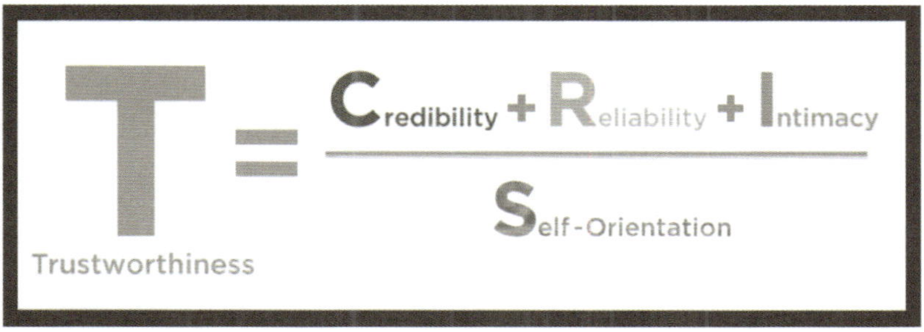


**Figure 7.1: The Trust Equation (Trusted Advisor Associates LLC, 2021).**

Let's walk through each variable of the equation and I'll explain how I work with leaders using this model.

### Trustworthiness

Remember what Blakey (2016:57) says: "You can choose to be trustworthy; you can work on it but only others can decide whether they trust you or not."

#### Reflection points

- What does it take to become worthy of the trust of others?
- What makes you trustworthy in the eyes of all your key stakeholders?

You can reflect on and elaborate on your answers to these questions but the answers will be in the components of the formula. As the adage goes: the devil is in the details.

### Credibility

Credibility is the words you speak. At the beginning of a relationship, your words bear more weight than your actions. As the relationship develops, reliability (another component) kicks in because your actions begin to bear more weight than your words. Sometimes it is easy to make promises, to say words, to manipulate data or information but when it comes to facing reality, words that are embellished can damage your reputation. Unfortunately, you are at risk of doing this when it comes to communicating through social media.

Credibility is also about your track record of past achievements (references, testimonials, certificates). It is about expertise, that you are knowledgeable, that you love your topic and can be passionate about it. Credibility is about your competence; how capable you are as a leader in the field of leadership. It is about people's accumulative and repeated positive experiences with you (another kind of track record), while you demonstrate that you are competent. People want you as their leader to be competent to guide them along the path to the future. You are not expected to be an expert in everything, rather you are expected to have a competent overall understanding of the market, the business, the organisation, and your people. You must understand the business impact of various fields of your company, be able to connect the dots and ask useful and insightful, smart questions. You cannot be expected to be technically competent in all operational specialities. Organisations are too complex and multifunctional for that. Don't make the mistake of interpreting your role as a leader to be, for instance, the greatest salesperson within your organisation. Your credibility as a leader shouldn't lay there. Your role is to hire the best salesperson with great future potential, to create an environment where the person can thrive, and to challenge and support them day after day to become better and better. Of course, this may mean that you occasionally have to admit that you don't know as much about something as your smartest team. However, never forget that you must do your homework to be at the level where you have an overall understanding of your business. You must also be knowledgeable about leading, something I rarely see. There are not enough leaders who have the daily habit of reading books about leadership and reflecting on them.

Credibility is also about your people saying that 'I can trust what you say, you don't hold me back, you don't manipulate the information, you don't exaggerate.' Be open, honest, transparent, and accurate in your communication.

Securing early wins in any leadership mandate will help you create momentum, and you will be perceived as a successful and credible leader in the short run. Nevertheless, there is a trap here. You can easily trade off your long-term credibility by focusing too much on the short-term benefits. Therefore, you must get it right. This is a balancing act. You should also consider and keep your eyes and focus on your long-term credibility at the cost of short-term gains and not the other way around.

### Reflection points

- What makes you credible as a leader in the eyes of your people?
- What makes you a credible leader in the eyes of your key stakeholders?
- How can you shift your credibility from subject matter expertise to leadership?

Remember, these elements of credibility are generic descriptions that should be further explored:

- What do they mean for you in your reality?
- For example, in your current position as a leader what track record of your past achievements/successes makes you (more) credible in the eyes of your people?

## Reliability

The second variable of the TRUST equation formula is reliability. Reliability is your actions, that anyone can trust you to do things, and that you always deliver great results. You set actionable and results-focused goals that can be measured. People trust you and follow you because you deliver, you produce, and they can rely on you in that respect. You don't just talk about what should be done but you show it, you demonstrate it. For example, you are a role model of accountability. From your own experience, you know that good leaders are consistent in doing what they said they would do for you; you can depend on them, as they will follow through.

Reliability is also about observable behaviours. What you expect of your people, you should role model with your behaviour so that everyone can see it.

Reliability is also about keeping deadlines, arriving at meetings on time, and giving a sense of security to others so that they can rely on you.

Your reputation as a leader is what people think of you, the opinions others have formed based on their experience with you. It is built up over time. The consequences of breaking promises are important. You not only need to keep your promise but consistently deliver what you promised. Remember the adage, under-promise and over-deliver? The problem with this thought is that you can surprise others, but the impact is negative in the long run as they won't know what to expect from you. I'm not saying you can't exceed expectations or be generous, but you may erode your trust if you keep surprising the other person and especially someone who really values consistency.

## *Consistency*

This word is not so trendy nowadays. I've heard many leaders say that it no longer makes them stand out, although it is essential. Why? Because consistency goes against flexibility, adaptability, and agility, the qualities leaders need to possess to remain competitive. But consistency still matters a lot. When I read *Developing the Leader within You 2.0* (Maxwell, 2018), it made me think.

Our world today puts more emphasis on creating magic with visibility, agility, adaptability, instant solutions, and quick wins instead of attending to our garden by laboriously nurturing plants like consistency and reliability. This picture sounds weird, doesn't it? Does magic always win over hard labour? This would be a very sad case for consistency. As one of the leaders I interviewed said:

> "When I always deliver what I promised, it is no longer attractive and no longer makes me stand out from my peers."

Nevertheless, after spending many years striving for consistency, the earnings can be extraordinary.

There is a prerequisite to consistency: self-discipline. Self-discipline makes consistency possible, otherwise, our performance fluctuates and is uneven, and our achievements are more accidental than sustainable.

### Consistency creates and shapes your reputation

Consistency makes people notice you. When you communicate the same messages, the same values, and the same qualities both verbally and non-verbally, after a while they will connect those messages, values, and qualities to you. This repetition becomes your leadership reputation.

**Consistency is a prerequisite to excellence**

Mastery of anything can only be achieved through the repetitive and intentional pursuit of actions in the chosen field for a long period. It doesn't happen overnight. It is hard work, a journey that has several phases. You can't skip any of those to jump straight to the top. You have to walk through it, learn through it, work hard through it with consistency. As I mentioned in Chapter II: C is for CREATIVITY and CREATE, being persistent and disciplined is essential to being creative and to further developing any talent of yours.

**Consistency provides security to others**

When people see your consistency, they can trust you more, they can predict your actions more, and they can rely on you more. Through your consistency, you provide them with a sense of stability and a circle of safety.

Leaders I interviewed highlight issues with predictability:

> "No matter whether you keep or don't keep your word, if you do it consistently, you are predictable. If you keep your words, and always deliver on what you have promised you are predictable and reliable."

> "Never keeping your word is better than sometimes keeping it, as your people would be able to better manage their emotional response. Because although it is ultimately negative, predictability gives them stability."

A similar dichotomy applies to the behavioural profiles of various leaders as well. Those leaders who have fragile profiles, i.e., they are easily readable but less flexible in behaviour and are more predictable; therefore, people can read them and adjust to them much more easily.

If the behavioural profile of a leader is very flexible, i.e., they can easily adapt to anyone but are therefore difficult to read, people may find it hard to rely on them.

As for predictability, another interviewed leader opened one more aspect to me about predictability. The problem with predictability is that although it is a good thing for creating stability, it can easily place the leader on a narrow path and they may get blindsided. From this point of view, predictability goes against the disruptive role of a leader, which is much needed for agility and creativity.

**Consistency reinforces corporate values and behaviours**

People do what people see. Leaders are behavioural role models in their organisation. When a leader cuts the corners, their people will cut the corners. If a leader shows up late, their people will show up late. So whatever behaviour the leader demonstrates consistently, their people will demonstrate that behaviour as well. That is the very reason why I keep telling leaders that everything within their organisation is about leadership and team interaction; they hold up a mirror to each other.

**Consistency multiplies**

"Successful people do daily what unsuccessful people do only occasionally" (Maxwell, 2018:201). When you decide to spend, say, an hour every day on your leadership development (e.g., reading books, articles, listening to podcasts, watching videos, reflecting, writing, attending coaching and training) it will add up to 7 hours per week, 30 hours per month, 365 hours per year, and 1,825 hours or 76 days per 5 years. Imagine how far you can get, how much you can achieve, and what impact you can have on others if (and if only) they watch your development, and even more if they come along with you.

### Reflection points

- What makes you a reliable leader?
- Where do you miss the power of role-modelling expected behaviours as a leader?
- What kind of reputation have you built as a leader?
- What reputation would you like to build as a leader?
- In which areas do you want to and decide to demonstrate consistency from now on? For example, pick one where winning may come easily, or identify one discipline you could practise to strengthen that area. Plan it, schedule it, and follow through consistently.
- In what areas do you demonstrate consistency or lack of consistency, perhaps unconsciously? Have a look at your daily routine, tiny habits, or your way of operating. They are full of data about you and how consistent you are.
- Who can provide you with feedback on your consistency or lack of consistency?

What happens when your words (credibility) and your actions (reliability) do not match? Incongruence, which first confuses your people, second shakes their trust. Then you may lose them.

## Intimacy (real human connection)

I prefer the phrase real human connection to the word intimacy. Because it is about connecting to people at a human-to-human level. It is about interpersonal connections, when you are really interested in your people. It happens when you want to know about them, their aspirations, their dreams, their ambitions, their fears, their concerns, their life. It is hard to get along with your people without getting to know them.

### Reflection points

- What do you know about your leadership team members, your key talents?
- What 2 or 3 non-business-related things do you know about each person?
- What does this person value?
- What are this person's top 3 concerns?
- What does this person want, hope, desire, dream, aspire for in life?

I could carry on. This is more challenging if you are very much task-focused; you naturally tend to connect with others mainly through tasks and achievable goals. The human-to-human level is about getting personal but not private, meaning you get to know the person without prying into their private life.

### *Transparency*

The dilemma of transparency is that you must weigh the advantages and importance of transparency against its disadvantages, limitations, and downsides. As we say in Hungary, *'Nem kellene átesni a ló másik oldalára'* so we should sit on the horse when it comes to transparency, i.e., avoid both extremes and find a middle ground. It has been clearly demonstrated in this technology-driven world that not all of us can handle transparency well. It can distort reality, heighten polarities, and it can be simply too much. Building transparency into your leadership, simply being honest and forthright about what is happening in the company now and in the future, is a difficult task. You can't fake it. You can't hide it for long. When you're a leader with integrity and your actions are driven by your values (which are hopefully in line with the organisational values), when you respect your fellow human, when you can make decisions, it is your responsibility to decide what level of transparency best serves the community, the common purpose.

It is much easier to be transparent for example with a small homogenous start-up company than with a big production company with a heterogeneous workforce. There is a limit to how much information you can share with all the employees; you need to decide where and how you need to differentiate your communication. It requires strong self-awareness to weigh whether you keep the information with yourself purely to be perceived as a strong and powerful leader, especially when there are so many unknown factors involved, or whether you take the mutual benefit of those you lead into consideration, sharing only that part of the information (not the whole) that helps people to move forward. Full transparency is a double-edged sword that leaders should use wisely.

### *Empathy: creating a humane environment*

First of all, it is your role as a leader to create an environment where your people feel safe to make mistakes through experimentation, to develop new skills, to admit mistakes let alone learn from them, and to be vulnerable and real. To achieve that, you should first have the courage to be vulnerable enough and real enough to admit that you make mistakes, to try new things, develop yourself and show how you learn from your mistakes. That is called vulnerability-based trust or getting naked figuratively (Lencioni, 2005). Do your people feel safe admitting their mistakes and sharing information with you? Do they feel they can open up with you?

The second most important thing when creating such an environment is to be trained to read between the lines, to detect and react to the emotions of your people by acknowledging emotions, frustration for example. Be able to put yourself in their shoes so that you can better understand their concerns and fears. See things from the perspectives of others. You should never embarrass them, neither face-to-face nor in front of others. You should respect them and approach them with good intentions and kindness from your heart. Because if you value your people, if you value their uniqueness, you increase your competitiveness and chances in the market.

## Self-orientation

The denominator in the formula is self-orientation, which is about self-centeredness. Here the ego can get in the way even if the intention and motives are good. Let me give you a typical example here. The intention as a leader is to always see possibilities and believe that most problems can be tackled with hard work and the right mindset. Say, the leader is a 'glass half full' kind of person. And their intention is to create the belief that the team can do it. They are so solution-focused that they cut the negative messages out of their communication with their team. For example, anything about problem identification, complaints, and emotions related to the difficulties they experience. The impact of this leader on the team can be that they undervalue the struggle the team is experiencing and the hard-fought learning and work they have put in. Employees may wonder if these types of leaders have lost their connection to reality, which may cause people to want to play it safe or not want to attempt hard things.

The other person needs to feel and say it internally: 'I trust them because they care about me.' High self-orientation brings down trustworthiness. The 'me, me, me' culture is the soil for this, when people show their importance for example by name dropping, by reciting their qualifications, by having the desire to be right, or to be seen to be right, or by having the tendency to relate their stories, because it is always about me, me, me.

Once I had a 'boss' at a multinational organisation, with whom I had to schedule one-to-one meetings regularly to brief her about the progress of my projects. It was typically an hour-long meeting. Usually, we spent 45 minutes of such a meeting with her telling me about how impactful and great she was when she conversed with certain leaders (I am reluctant to use the word 'work' here as she did not do anything, just talked). She dropped the names of big regional leaders to see how impressed I was by her greatness and importance. Then I had to listen to and empathetically respond to all the frustrations she had living in a foreign country. I had only 15 minutes of every booked one-hour meeting to talk about my tasks, my challenges, my concerns, and my questions. I am reluctant to call her a leader and prefer to use the term 'boss' with every negative connotation it has.

Your people's perception about whether you care or don't care about them matters a lot. Again, if you are overly task-focused you may come across as someone who doesn't care about their people, only about their tasks. Your conversation with people, if you want to build trusted relationships, should be either balanced or less about your agenda and more about theirs. When you are working from your agenda, you want to solve the other person's problems quickly to meet your needs. You talk because you need to and want to. You make assumptions and don't check them with the other person. The conversation becomes about your emotional state. You interrupt the other person with your own concerns. The work and interaction are at your preferred pace, and even if you ask questions, you only do it to satisfy your need for information.

When you pay attention to the other person's agenda, you listen to understand instead of listening to respond. You check your assumptions and interpretations to better understand. You are interested in the other person and what the other person has to say. You move at their pace, using questions to deepen your understanding of their issues and finally you pay attention to their feelings.

You need to move from self-orientation to service-orientation, where your focus is more on others, on serving others, helping them be the best version of themselves and, therefore, achieving better results for the organisation and the team. It is not about neglecting yourself; this whole book is about focusing on yourself as a leader and paying attention to when and where you need to shift your focus from self to others intentionally. "Service orientation for a leader manifests in four crucial ways: service to your leaders, service to your team, service to your customers, and service to yourself" (Morgan, 2020:151). Think beyond yourself. Choose to be humble. Exhibiting selflessness is essential for serving others.

All these require you to talk less, ask questions, listen actively, and check understanding.

### *When you change how you listen, you'll change everything*

The success of modern leadership depends more and more on the ability of the leader to observe their quality of listening and to adjust the quality of listening to what is needed in each situation. How much attention do you pay to your listening? Are you listening to understand or to respond?

Listening is probably the most underrated leadership skill. It is the least taught but most used skill. The biggest leadership failures come from leaders being unable to connect with and make sense of the VUCA world around them.

If you value the other person, you should be open to their thoughts, opinions, and perspectives. The ratio of trustworthiness very much depends on your ability to actively listen to your people and hear what they have to say and respond timely and adequately.

Four levels of listening (based on Scharmer, 2018):

1. **Downloading or selective listening:** Listening is limited to reconfirming what we already know. Nothing new penetrates our bubble. It is about us. We pay more attention to our own judgements, opinions, and interpretation and drive our own agenda. It is about listening to respond.

2. **Factual listening:** We let the data talk to us and notice disconfirming information. Doing this requires opening the mind, i.e., the capacity to suspend our habits of judgement. It is pretty much listening to the words and facts of what is being said by the other person.

3. **Empathic listening:** We see the situation through the eyes of another. Doing this requires opening the heart, using our feelings and our heart as an organ to tune in to another person's view. We listen to the other person's expression, emotions, and everything they bring. We notice not only what they say but how they say it. We notice what they don't say and what is between the lines. "Switching on" our hearts in this way helps us activate our source of empathic listening.
4. **Generative or global listening:** We listen for the highest future possibility to show up while holding a space for something new to be born. It is the deepest and highest of listening involving all our senses, our intuition, our gut feeling, and all the meta-views. It is the most challenging. It is something that we cannot force. We can create conditions for generative/global listening. The most important intervention at this level is this: Do nothing. Do not intervene. Do not disengage. Just stay with and hold the space for what wants to emerge.

Based on this, when you listen on level 1 'downloading', your attention is not focused on what the other person says but on your own inner dialogue or commentary. For example, you may be planning what you will say next. As you cross the threshold from downloading to factual listening (level 1 to 2), your attention moves from listening to your inner voice to actually listening to the person in front of you. You open up to what is being said. When you start to cross the threshold from factual to empathic listening (level 2 to 3), your place of listening shifts from you to the other person, i.e., from your small vehicle (the intelligence of your head) to your larger vehicle (the intelligence of your heart). You step into the other person's perspective. For example, you might think, 'Oh, I may not agree, but I can see how they see this situation.' Finally, when you cross the threshold from empathic to global listening (level 3 to 4), your listening becomes a holding space for bringing something new into a reality that wants to be born. You listen with openness to what is unknown and emerging.

You do and should use all levels of listening even within a conversation. All of them are appropriate in one situation or another. The success of your leadership and change depends on your ability to observe your quality of listening and to adjust the quality of listening to what is needed in each situation.

Barriers to active listening:

- Voice of judgement
- Voice of cynicism
- Voice of fear

Shifting how you listen, and the way you pay attention sounds like a really small change. But here's the thing. Changing how you listen means that you change how you experience relationships and the world. And if you change that, you change, well, everything.

### Exercise #1

At the end of each day, spend 5 minutes reviewing how you engaged in empathic listening (open mind and heart) and global/ generative listening (open mind, heart, and will). If you can't identify a single instance of deep listening, take note of that, too. If you do this exercise for a month, your effectiveness as a listener will rise dramatically. All it takes is the discipline to conduct that 5-minute review process every day. And if possible, try to find 2 or 3 colleagues who will do the same thing and share your experiences.

### Exercise #2

What is the voice in your head (the little (wo)man) saying? If it is judgement, you have a closed mind. If it is cynicism, you have a closed heart. If it is fear, you have a closed will.

## TRUST in economic terms

Covey (2008) talks about trust in economic terms. This is another formula-based dimension of trust I like exploring with leaders. Trust always affects two outcomes: speed and cost. The higher the trust in the organisation the quicker the organisation can respond to both internal and external needs, so the higher the speed is, the lower the related costs incurred are. If trust diminishes, speed will also decrease and that will cost much more. So, distrust costs a lot. Therefore, it is very important to build trust in your organisation intentionally and systematically.

Having conversations with leaders about where they lose time in the organisation, where they are too slow, what takes up more time, where collaboration requires more effort and time than needed, shows where they lack trust in the organisation.

## TRUST in emotional terms

The other economic term I like using is the Emotional Bank Account (Covey, 2004). We make conscious decisions related to our finances every day; we make deposits, save money, and when needed, we withdraw money from our bank account. Unfortunately, we tend to pay very little attention to our emotional bank account, where we have a ledger of deposits and withdrawals for our relationship bank account as well. Each relationship can be viewed through this lens. When the balance is high, the level of trust is high as well. When the balance is low, trust plummets, and the relationship suffers.

There are ways you can make deposits that can help you build trusted relationships: keep your commitments, do little things, especially particular things you don't have to do for the other person, listen empathically particularly when the other person needs emotional support and so on. When you make mistakes or let down the other person or ask for support, you withdraw amounts from the emotional bank account from time to time. When you withdraw a lot and don't make any deposit, sooner or later, the other person will not want to have any relationship with you. You may come across as a calculating person.

If you neglect your emotional bank account, you can create a lack of equality and unbalance in the relationship. The whole system is based on reciprocity. Take 100% responsibility for making the relationship work with your key stakeholders. Don't assume or expect. Take the first steps to learn about their priorities and goals. Using the trust equation and the emotional bank account you can build trust intentionally with your key stakeholders.

## TRUST others – one to many: organisations and networks

How can you create an environment in which teams trust each other, and are fully engaged with their heads and hearts?

A high-performing team is when team members look out for each other and turn to each other for support and empathy. They work not only for their own goals or common goals but also for the success of others. When you as a leader create an environment for the free flow of information, people feel they will do whatever it takes to succeed and that you help them succeed. You as a leader have two roles: to role model trust, and to create a high-trust, safe environment where people can learn and perform.

One of the challenges is to get the right balance between individual and team goals. When there is too much focus on individual goals, internal rivalries intensify, which can shatter any culture. Unhealthy internal competition can poison an organisational culture because it places the focus and energy in the wrong place; people spend way too much time protecting themselves from others instead of hunting for new clients on the market.

Too much individualism can kill cooperation and a trustful environment. It shouldn't be the case. I like the example of a jazz band, where the 'me' and 'we' cultures come together. There is high cooperation in a jazz band. Band members appreciate each other's talents; musicians take turns stepping out, while the others support the soloist from the back. Then that soloist takes a step back to support the next soloist. There are occasions when the whole band plays together, and there are occasions when each member has the opportunity to shine and lead while the others support and follow. This requires a fluid structure with some specific rules to trust and respect each other's talent and make the team successful as a whole.

If an organisation is mostly task-focused, all the interaction is based on tasks. There is no place for social interaction, which is important to build trust. In such cases, you, as a leader, need to focus more on creating opportunities for team members to have less-formal, social interactions.

Building trust creates a safe environment where issues and differences can be openly discussed, and where the status quo can be challenged. You as a leader build trust for cooperative conversations, during which information and feedback flow smoothly.

The consequences of the lack of trust in organisations, which you must bear in mind, are high turnover, lack of engagement, lack of ownership, and half-hearted employees due to lack of buy-in. And, it costs money, because everything takes longer.

## Internal and external network building

Intentional and consistent network building is usually at the end of the to-do lists of many leaders. However, the power of social networks, i.e., who you know, is highly valuable to you as a leader and can become an incredible asset to any leadership candidate or during your transition to the C-Suite.

Leaders, including you, are in the public eye more than ever before; shareholders and key stakeholders want answers about and insights into what the organisation is doing. Being able to communicate in this world is essential. Interact with many stakeholders, build trust with them, and be aware of how you communicate.

You don't need to know everything. And frankly speaking, you can't possess everything it takes to lead an organisation. You need to know the people who can help, who have the knowledge. You need to know people who know the people who can help. When you lose yourself in the day-to-day operations, you can easily lose the external perspective of this power. Train yourself to see the value of knowing people (both internally and externally) and have a real connection with them. To build a network through real human connections, you have to invest time and energy. Do your homework and your research on the person. Read everything about them or everything written by them. Carefully think through the questions you want to ask. Let your enthusiasm, your curiosity, and even your passion shine through during the meeting. Don't play games; if you do, there will be no real connection. Learn as much as possible, not only about the person and your common interest but from the person as well. Why is this so important? Because interested people are interesting. It will pay off for you. It is how you can build and sustain alliances both internally and externally.

Once I had a conversation with a director, for whom network building was a pain. We talked a lot about how he could approach it. I want to highlight two of his key learning points: 1) Everyone needs to eat, it is vital to our biological existence, so why not do it with others as part of network building; 2) Create a list of topics you like to discuss other than business. Many introvert leaders find it challenging to connect on a human-to-human level as it is outside the expert content they feel comfortable with.

**Draw up your own networking plan and be conscious about it. Consistency is more important than intensity.**

Leaders spend way too much time focusing on vertical relationships up to the boss and down to direct reports and not enough on peers and other stakeholders.

Identify your key stakeholders, both current and potential. Categorise them. Who are the supporters, the alliances, the opponents, the influencers, the decision-makers, the informers, and perhaps the accidental saboteurs? What do they need from you? What do you need from them? This is also the way you can meet and learn about your future customers and employees: what their needs are, what their expectations are, what they want to know about you and your business. Have formal or less formal conversations. This is the only way you can learn to speak and use their language. Discipline yourself to invest in building up relationship bank accounts with people internally and externally. Build alliances. Map the influencing landscape. Note who will be the most important for your success, who are the key decision-makers, and who are the formal or more importantly the informal influencers? Reciprocity is a strong social norm. A well-balanced emotional bank account is key. Who are the people potentially blocking alliances? Who are the ones who collectively have the power to say no? How can you neutralise them?

Where do you need to build your networks to expand your capacity and compensate for blind spots and gaps in your own expertise or experience? Think of your vulnerabilities and weaknesses. How will you compensate for them? Business is not only a people business but also a team game.

Understand the shadow organisation, the informal set of processes and alliances that exist in the shadow of the formal structure, which strongly influences how work actually gets done. How can you best utilise it? Remember, this is not something that should be diminished; that will never happen. It is something you can turn to your advantage and to the advantage of your organisation.

## TRUST in the unknown

In this VUCA world, there are so many unknown elements of any story. We experience information overload every day. We must decide what is the truth or what information we need to make the best decision. It is overly messy. And there is a fierce, sometimes bloody competition out there.

You may feel that you need to give the benefit of the doubt on way too many occasions. But what you need is to have faith and trust that, based on the overwhelming yet scattered information you have, you will make the best decision. You as a leader also must trust the future, drive your company into the unknown, and manage the gaps between risks known today and the unknown risks of tomorrow. Ask questions to explore as many hypotheses and scenarios as possible. When there are no unknowns we can guarantee an outcome, so the risk is low. However, today's world is full of uncertainties. Still, all your key stakeholders want reassurance from you to bring the best out of any situation that affects them. When it comes to trusting the future, it is really about trusting yourself and your organisation that whatever happens, you will tackle the problem and get the most and the best out of it. How can you do it? Prepare yourself and your organisation as much as possible.

A leader who does not work on themselves to prepare for the future will not be able to prepare their organisation for the future and will inevitably fall behind rather quickly.

What else do you need? Trust in yourself, your capabilities, your native genius, your creativity, and your uniqueness. And trust your team, that together you can conquer whatever comes up.

Today, you and all leaders are also experiencing hardship and adversity filled with the unknown and uncertainty due to the global pandemic and the world economic recession. It not only puts you under enormous pressure but also provides an opportunity to learn more about yourself and each other. How you and others handle problems in such difficult times tells you a lot about who you are and who they are. You truly get to know a person through adversity.

## TRUST in gratitude

Real and authentic gratitude from the heart is a feeling that makes relationships stronger because it requires you to see how you have been supported, strengthened, and empowered by other people. It is one of the most underutilised and powerful tools in the leadership toolbox.

Living with gratitude requires that you consciously and daily affirm the goodness in your life. It elevates you and can be leveraged in both your family and circle of friends and of course in your organisation.

Using a gratitude journal, or a more playful tool called a gratitude jar, should be a must for any leader. Why? Because you learn to appreciate how far you got with the help of others, how important it is to see the value in what you do and how you do it. And what value others can bring to you. You learn to value yourself and others as beautifully unique creators of your joint stories.

Leaders who practice gratitude regularly will see and appreciate others more than those who do not.

## Reflection points

- Who are your key stakeholders both internally and externally? Create a list.
- How can you describe each relationship? What do they look like? What do you need from each person? What does the person need from you?
- Think through this list based on the Emotional Bank Account concept (debits and credits).
- Add potential clients, decision-makers, influencers, and teachers (who will help you grow) to that list.
- Plan a breakfast/lunch and a lunch/dinner with two people and calls/mail exchange with two people every week. Be consistent; it will compound. Be inspirational for and inspired by others.
- Create your gratitude journal. Write down 2 things and people you are grateful for every single day in your journal or on a Post-it and put it into a gratitude jar. The icing on the cake here is to review your gratitude notes on 31 December and enter into the New Year with elevated energy and a smile on your face and in your heart.

# CHAPTER VII

## Inside Journey - the leader in you What makes you a unique and powerful leader?

"Each bird must sing with its own throat."

(Ibsen, cited in Johnson, 2015)

## Pulling it all together - What is your CRAFT?

### The CRAFT Leadership model

Sharpening the REAL LEADER in you not only means connecting and reconnecting to your REAL self as a leader but it also means continuously developing and creating a shift in the CRAFT Leadership qualities. To meet the challenges of the unpredictable and continuously changing business environment, leaders must possess these 5 leadership qualities: CREATIVITY, RESILIENCE, AGILITY, FOCUS, and TRUST (Figure 8.1).

**Figure 8.1: CRAFT Leadership (Source: Author's own).**

The answers to the questions raised at the very end of this chapter are the pinnacle of your CRAFT journey in terms of who you are and what you stand for as a leader.

But before that, let's recap on what you have read so far in this book and do an inventory of where you are on your CRAFT Leadership journey.

This is an opportunity to revisit what you have read and learnt about the 5 CRAFT Leadership qualities in a one-page summary, a mind-map. After re-examining the reflection questions you read in each chapter, you can do a self-assessment to learn where you stand with each of the 5 qualities.

## CRAFT Leadership mind maps

Each mind map will visually outline the summary of key points to remember for each chapter. It will help you quickly oversee where you stand on your journey for each quality to master CRAFT Leadership.

## CRAFT Leadership summary of reflection questions

I have collected all the questions asked in each chapter to enable you to re-examine your answers to those questions.

## CRAFT Leadership self-assessment

The self-assessment part will help you to better understand where you are on your CRAFT Leadership journey. It helps you identify areas where you are more or less effective in the 5 CRAFT Leadership qualities and where you need to further sharpen your skills to become the leader you wish to be.

The self-assessment section lists 10 statements for each quality. Read each statement carefully. Place a checkmark next to each one that you agree is true for you. Answer using your first instinct. Please don't skip any of it and don't go back to change any of your first responses.

## CREATIVITY and CREATE Mind Map

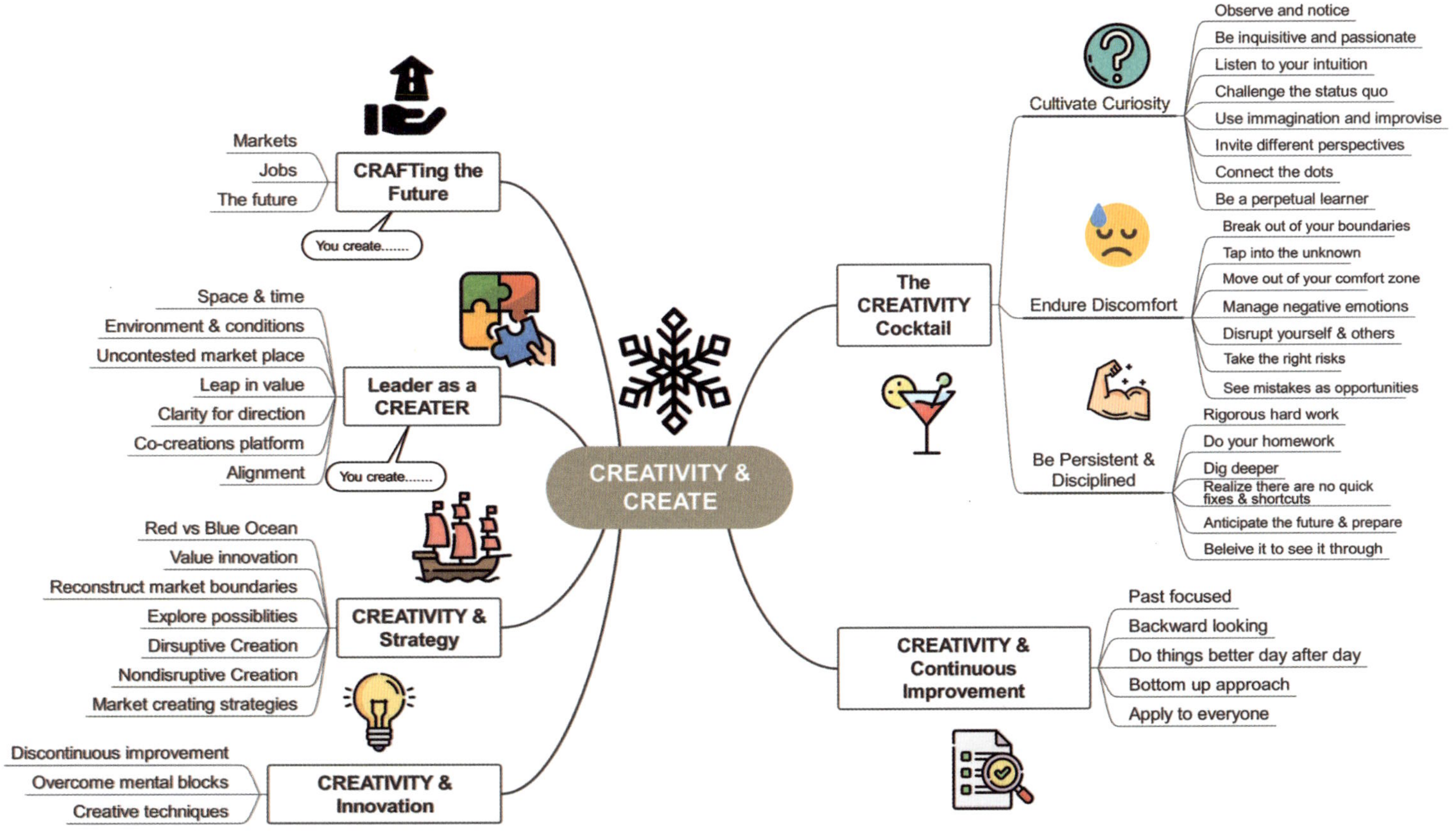

## CREATIVITY and CREATE – Summary of Reflection Questions

- Which ingredient of the Creativity cocktail is over- or under-represented in your leadership team, in your organisation (cultivate curiosity, endure discomfort, be persistent and disciplined)? Revisit Chapter II: C is for CREATIVITY and CREATE if you would like to check what falls under each ingredient of the Creativity cocktail and answer further questions to dig deeper.
- What kind of organisation do you want to build?
- What kind of future do you want to create and how are you going to do it?
- How can you introduce novelty into your organisation?
- How can you make your people think more out of the box, and generate novel and useful ideas?
- How can you create an environment in your organisation where there is a place and process for discontinuous improvement, creativity, and innovation?
- Where is your business reality?
- In which direction are you sailing your craft?
- How much do you sail on the Red Ocean and how much on the Blue Ocean?
- How bloody is your Red Ocean? What are the weather conditions?
- How could you focus more on the Blue Ocean instead of the Red Ocean?
- How do you steer your craft?
- What kind of craft do you have?

- Create a list of key factors your industry currently competes on. Which of the factors that the industry takes for granted should be eliminated?
- Which factors should be reduced well below the industry's standard?
- Which factors should be raised well above the industry's standard?
- Which factors that the industry has never offered should be created?

## CREATIVITY and CREATE – Self-Assessment

| |
|---|
| ☐ I have a clear picture of where I and my leadership team stand (strengths and weaknesses) with the 3 ingredients of the CREATIVITY cocktail (cultivate curiosity, endure discomfort, be persistent and disciplined). |
| ☐ I role model and encourage everyone on my leadership team to continuously improve themselves and the work they do and expect the same from their teams as well. |
| ☐ I initiate and create platforms (time and space) and conditions for creativity and innovation. |
| ☐ I continuously search the market (micro and macro level) and generate discussion within my leadership team about new, yet unknown possibilities for the organisation. |
| ☐ I always search to see how I can connect the unconnected to create new. |
| ☐ I not only recognise and incentivise opportunities for added value creation but value innovation as well within and outside the organisation. |

| |
|---|
| ☐ Every week I intentionally create causes and platforms for co-creation within the organisation where I bring people with different perspectives to the table. |
| ☐ I expect my leadership team to challenge the status quo and bring new questions to the table. |
| ☐ I keep in mind that my role as a leader is not only about profit but about people and the planet as well; therefore, I make sure that I create jobs and make conscious efforts to create and lead a sustainable company. |
| ☐ Every day I train myself and take responsibility to craft the future for not only myself but for all the people I am responsible for. |

If you marked 8 or more of these statements as true for you, then you have probably mastered this quality.

Note the unmarked statements that you could still work on to further enhance this quality.

Write down the areas you want to work on based on the unmarked statements. Select the 20% that brings you 80% results!

........................................................................................................

........................................................................................................

........................................................................................................

........................................................................................................

Which statements did you find hard to respond to? Consider asking others for feedback.

........................................................................................................

........................................................................................................

........................................................................................................

........................................................................................................

## RESILIENCE Mind Map

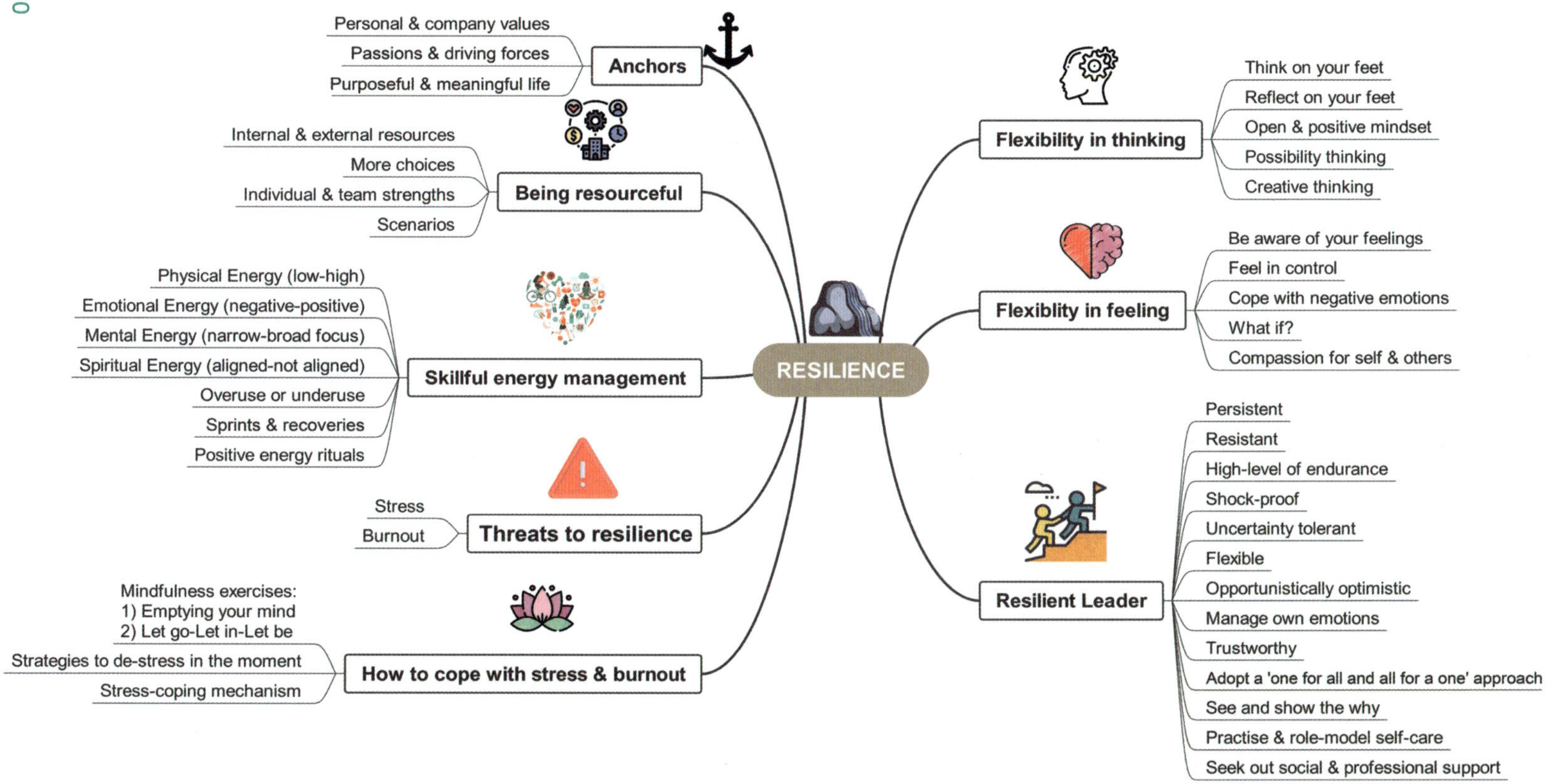

## RESILIENCE – Summary of Reflection Questions

- What is your approach to the unexpected? How do you respond to stress? How do you manage the inner and outer turbulence of today's world?
- Can you survive setbacks? Can you work through adversity?
- As a leader, how do you prevent yourself from getting fatigued or burnt out?
- Do you have an energy budget?
- What does resilience mean for you as a leader?
- As a leader, when do you need to stand like a rock and when do you need to swim with the current?
- As a leader, how valuable would it be to bring more positive energy and passion to your organisation?
- If those you lead would bring more positive energy into the workplace, how would it affect their relationships with their colleagues and the quality of service that they deliver to customers and clients?
- To deliver high performance, to bring out the best in you, to perform at your maximum level for an extended period, you need lots of energy. As a leader, how do you take control of your energy budget?
- Where do you leak energy and where do you gain energy during work?
- How are you spending your energy now?
- How can you keep performing at your best without sacrificing your health, your happiness, and your passion for life?

- In which of the 4 areas (physical, emotional, mental, and spiritual) do you feel the most deficit?
- What does your energy budget look like? When was the last time you considered the overuse or underuse of your energy capacity?

## RESILIENCE – Self-Assessment

| |
|---|
| ☐ I honour my personal values and corporate values every day by my words and actions. |
| ☐ People can see and have positive experiences about how passionate I am about leading teams and the organisation. |
| ☐ I am a resourceful leader. I have and consider many choices, scenarios, internal and external resources, and strengths for me and my teams. |
| ☐ I am flexible in my thinking by frequently reflecting on how I lead, possessing a positive mindset, and using possibility and creative thinking. |
| ☐ People see me as a leader who is fully aware of the emotional side of the business, copes well with negative emotions, and cares about and responds to their feelings with empathy and compassion. |
| ☐ I have weekly and daily rituals and routines in place to avoid stress and burn-out. |
| ☐ I consciously and skilfully manage my energy at all levels (physical, emotional, mental, and spiritual). |
| ☐ I recognise and correct when I overuse or underuse any of my energy sources or those of the organisation I lead. |

| |
|---|
| ☐ I believe that practising self-care is not a selfish act; it has a tremendous effect on those I lead, as I am the steward of the organisation's energy. Therefore, I have my own self-care programme. |
| ☐ I believe a sustainable organisation has skilful energy management. Therefore, I make sure that the people under my responsibility have the opportunity to recover after the heavy sprints in today's fast-moving business world. |

If you marked 8 or more of these statements as true for you, then you have probably mastered this quality.

Note the unmarked statements you could still work on to further enhance this quality.

Write down the areas you want to work on based on the unmarked statements. Select the 20% that brings you 80% results!

.................................................................................................

.................................................................................................

.................................................................................................

.................................................................................................

Which statements did you find hard to respond to? Consider asking others for feedback.

.................................................................................................

.................................................................................................

.................................................................................................

.................................................................................................

## AGILITY Mind Map

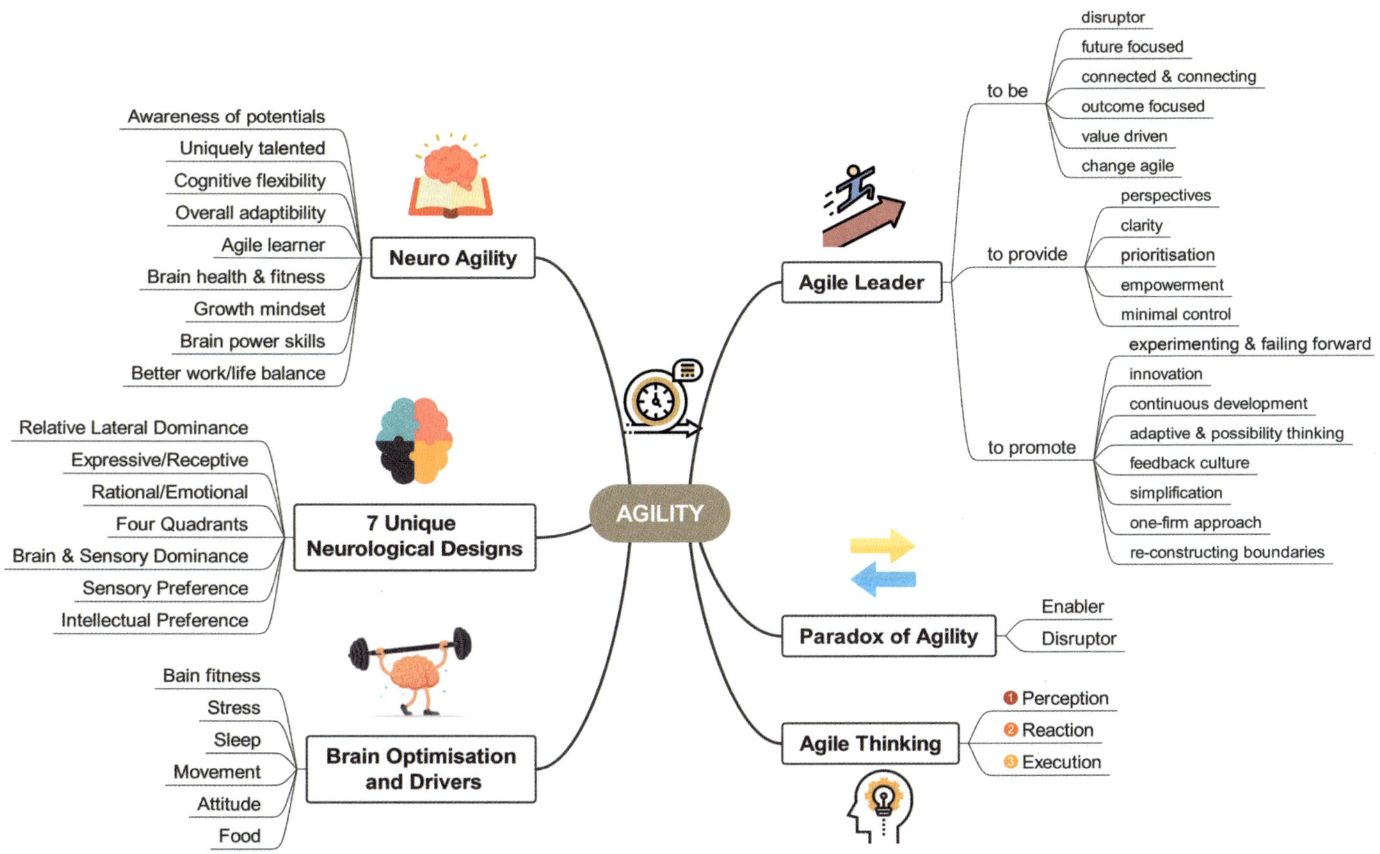

## AGILITY – Summary of Reflection Questions

- Every team's definition of agile differs as each team is very different in every single business. Yet agility differs for every organisation. What does agility mean for you, for your team, and for your organisation?
- Why is agility important (if so) and how can you make it happen as a leader?
- What is your role as a leader in it?
- Look at each item on the Agile Leader Characteristics list (page 139). Mark those that you are absolutely sure about as an integral part of your leadership. Write down pieces of evidence, i.e., two concrete examples for each item you opted for. Be as detailed and specific as possible. Then have a look at those that are not part of your leadership, the ones you have not marked. How many remain on your list?
- To what extent do you need to develop them and how can they help you lead your organisation from good to great?
- What can you do to start implementing them? Commit to 3 to 4 small action points and follow them through.
- How do you think the 6 brain optimisation drivers influence your brain health?
- How do you think these drivers impact your performance?
- In which areas do you still need to develop further?
- What is your plan of action to optimise your brain performance?

## AGILITY – Self-Assessment

- ☐ I am fully aware of my strengths and weaknesses in being an Agile Leader.
- ☐ I intentionally disrupt myself and my organisation before being disrupted by external forces.
- ☐ I always challenge the status-quo and seek opportunities to invite new methods, solutions, and thinking into our day-to-day operations.
- ☐ I empower my people to solve problems and make decisions to be able to quickly respond to the needs of clients and the market.
- ☐ I continuously develop and renew myself and my organisation or my team to adapt to today's volatile business environment.
- ☐ I oversee complex problems and process a vast amount of information quickly.
- ☐ I have a growth mindset; I see opportunities in every challenge, continuously learn, and am open to giving and receiving regular feedback.
- ☐ I am open to learning more about my own neurological design to better understand how I learn, how I process information, and how I think and make decisions quickly.
- ☐ I consciously and intentionally pay attention to the 6 drivers that help optimise my brain (brain fitness, stress, sleep, movement, attitude, and food).
- ☐ I am close to my clients to better understand how their needs are changing.

If you marked 8 or more of these statements as true for you, then you have probably mastered this quality.

Note the unmarked statements that you could still work on to further enhance this quality.

Write down the areas you want to work on based on the unmarked statements. Select the 20% that brings you 80% results!

..........................................................................................................

..........................................................................................................

..........................................................................................................

..........................................................................................................

Which statements did you find hard to respond to? Consider asking others for feedback.

..........................................................................................................

..........................................................................................................

..........................................................................................................

..........................................................................................................

## FOCUS Mind Map

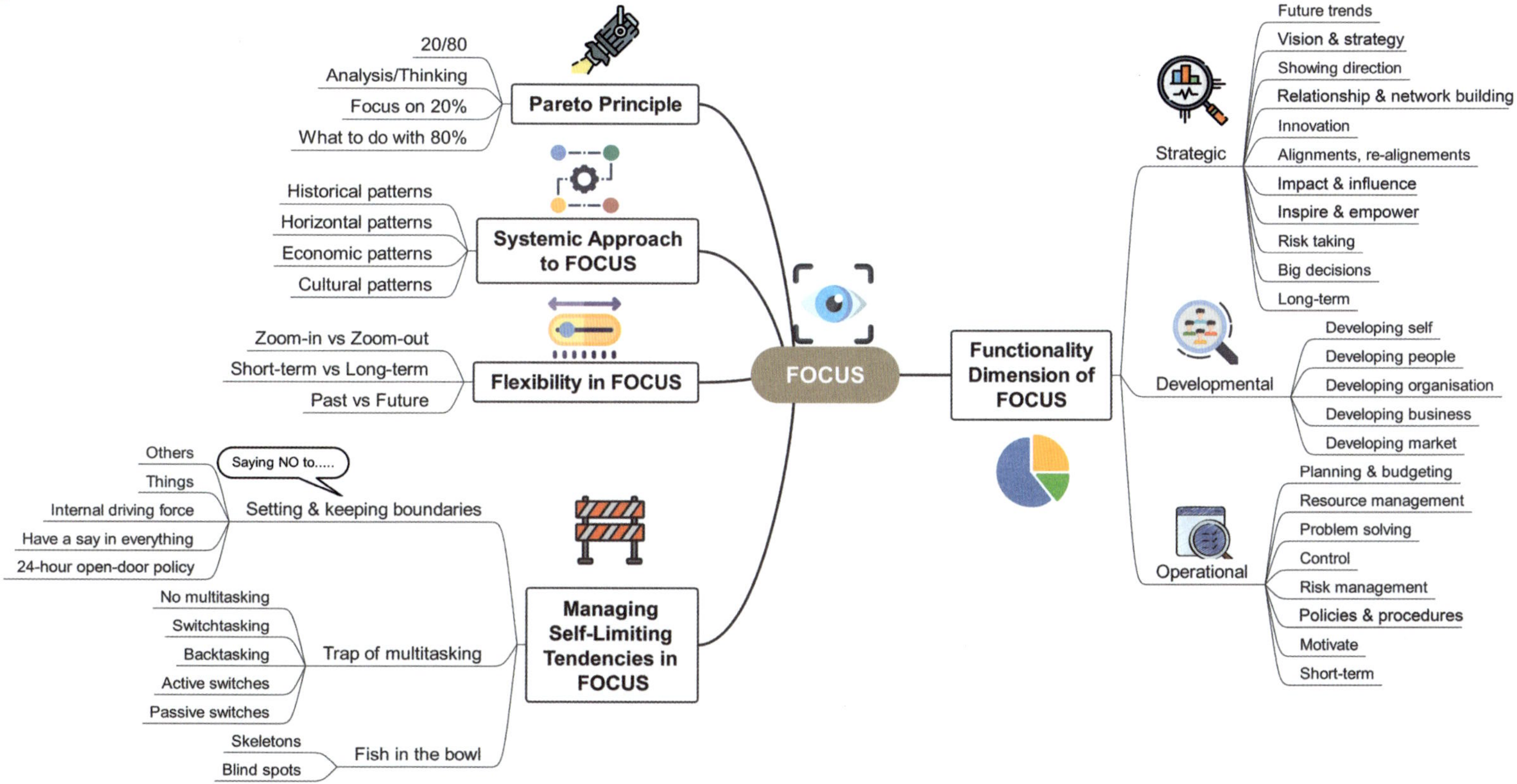

## FOCUS – Summary of Reflection Questions

- Where do you have your focus right now?
- Where do you want to put the spotlight on?
- What happens when you lose focus?
- What are the consequences, the positive and negative impacts of your losing focus?
- Where do you need to sharpen yourself to gain mastery in this leadership quality?
- How is your time allocated between the 3 leadership domains: strategic, developmental, and operational?
- Do you constantly ask yourself what is the 20% here that is leading me to the 80%?
- What is preventing you and your teams from focusing on the 20%?
- Who are the top 20% of your people you should focus on?
- Where and how can you use the Pareto Principle in your day-to-day activity, in your client portfolio, and in your leadership?
- If tomorrow's 20% (tasks, events, focus) will be different from today's 20%, where will they come from?
- What patterns can you recognise in the history of your organisation before you embark on a new change?
- What cultural patterns emerge if you look at the last 4 employee engagement surveys of your organisation?
- Through systemic lenses, what patterns can you detect in the information you are receiving?
- Where do your teams work seamlessly across the organisation?
- Where do you see tensions and detachments that undermine performance?

- How can you master flexibility in your leadership FOCUS?
- Learn what are your natural tendencies. Where do you feel more comfortable (in zoom-in or zoom-out mode, short-term activities or long-term activities, to build on the past or build on the future)? And what are the consequences of neglecting the other end of each range?
- Be aware of how much energy is required from you in moving across these ranges. Where do you leak the most energy?
- What conscious effort or personal system do you need to put in place to keep your focus and at the same time be flexible?
- What controlling questions do you need to ask? When and where do you need to change your controlling questions as data may get distorted?
- What are you not seeing, not noticing?
- What are you missing? What do you need?
- Whose perception/lens do you need to borrow?
- How can you uncover your leadership blind spots? Who can help you with that? What are your organisation's blind spots?
- When and to what extent do people seek you out, avoid you, or work around you?
- Where do you neglect your own boundaries? Where do you let others take advantage of you?
- Where do you find it difficult to say NO?
- To whom do you find it difficult to say NO?
- What do you find difficult to say NO to?
- What systems and rules do you need to say NO to more in all these areas?

## FOCUS – Self-Assessment

| |
|---|
| ☐ I spend most of my time and effort on the strategic and developmental domain as a leader. |
| ☐ I spend the least amount of my time on operational tasks compared to the other two domains (strategic and developmental). |
| ☐ I focus on the 20% of my tasks that bring 80% results, success, and impact. |
| ☐ I make sure that I delegate, drop, or deliver the minimum viable solutions in 80% of my tasks that bring 20% results, success, and impact. |
| ☐ Most of the problems that occur in my organisation are solved by my managers and my teams. I mainly solve problems at a systemic level. |
| ☐ I easily flex my focus between zoom-in and zoom-out, short-term and long-term, and past and future. |
| ☐ I spend more time on zoom-out than zoom-in, long-term than short-term, and future than past. |
| ☐ I am firmly setting and keeping my boundaries and I encourage others to do so. I can say NO to urges, things, and people without damaging the relationship and the positive results. |
| ☐ I believe that multitasking is a lie and causes more distraction in the workflow than help. |
| ☐ I always watch out for blind spots and skeletons in my organisation. I ask questions that help uncover them. |

If you marked 8 or more of these statements as true for you, then you have probably mastered this quality.

Note the unmarked statements that you could still work on further to enhance this quality.

Write down the areas you want to work on based on the unmarked statements. Select the 20% that brings you 80% results!

.......................................................................................................

.......................................................................................................

.......................................................................................................

.......................................................................................................

.......................................................................................................

Which statements did you find hard to respond to? Consider asking others for feedback.

.......................................................................................................

.......................................................................................................

.......................................................................................................

.......................................................................................................

.......................................................................................................

## TRUST Mind Map

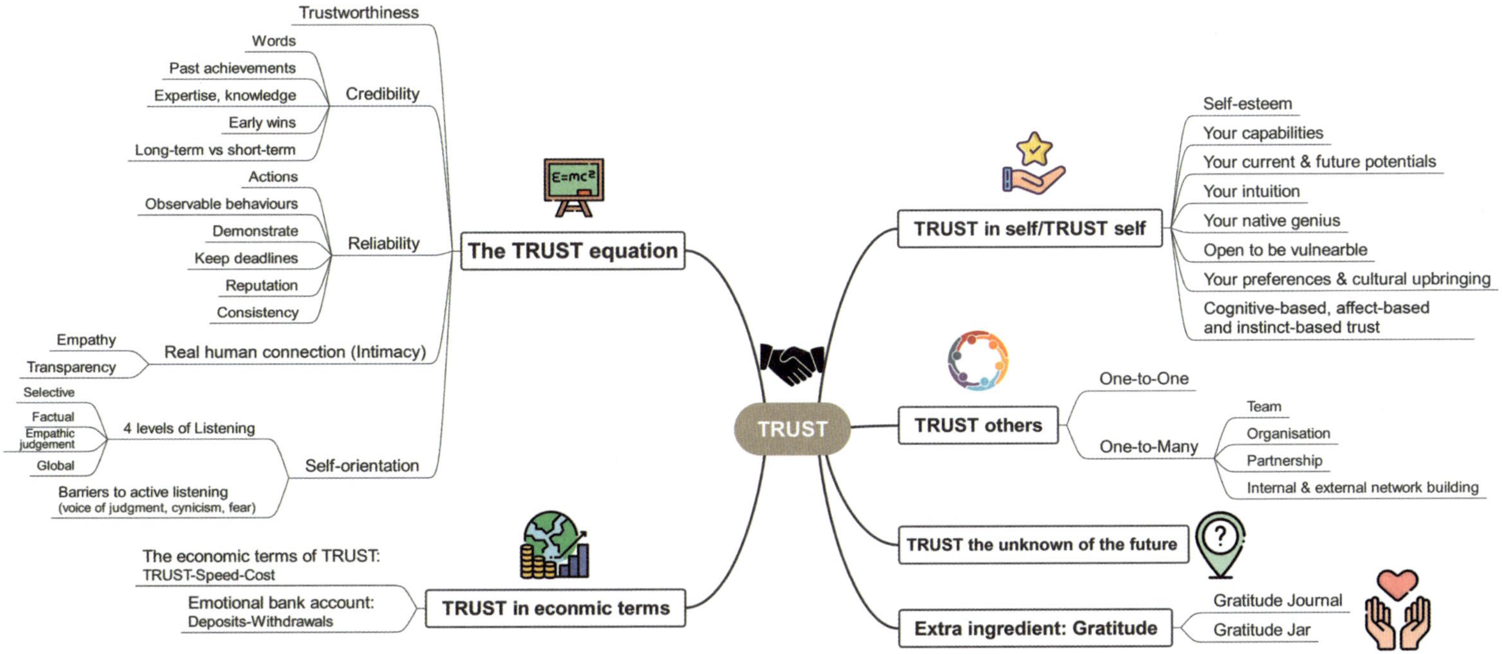

## TRUST – Summary of Reflection Questions

- What is your natural trust source (head, heart, or gut)? How much do you let your heart and gut influence your leadership style?
- How often do you listen to your intuition when you make a business or a people-related decision?
- When was the last time you admitted that you had made a mistake in front of others? What was your key learning about yourself? Have you shared your key learning?
- Inner critic checking: What does the little voice in your head (your inner critic) keep telling you about yourself? What is it saying? Where are these views coming from and why? How is it affecting your day-to-day work, your relationships, and your performance? How can you turn down your inner critic's voice?
- What does it take to become worthy of the trust of others?
- What makes you trustworthy in the eyes of all your key stakeholders?
- What makes you credible as a leader in the eyes of your people?
- What makes you a credible leader in the eyes of your key stakeholders?
- How can you shift your credibility from subject matter expertise to leadership?
- Remember these elements of credibility are generic descriptions that should be further explored: What do they mean for you in your reality? For example, in your current position as a leader, what track record of your past achievements/successes makes you (more) credible in the eyes of your people?
- What makes you a reliable leader?

- Where do you miss the power of role-modelling expected behaviours as a leader?
- What kind of reputation have you built as a leader? What reputation would you like to build as a leader?
- In which areas do you want and decide to demonstrate consistency from now on? For example, pick one where winning may come easily, or identify one discipline you could practise to strengthen that area. Plan it, schedule it, and follow through consistently.
- In what areas do you demonstrate consistency or lack of consistency, maybe unconsciously? Have a look at your daily routine, tiny habits, or your way of operating. They are full of data about you and how consistent you are.
- Who can provide you with feedback on your consistency efforts or lack of consistency?
- What do you know about your leadership team members, your key talents?
- What 2 or 3 non-business-related things do you know about the person?
- What does this person value?
- What are their top 3 concerns?
- What do they want, hope, desire, dream, aspire for in life?
- How much attention do you pay to listening to people? Are you listening to understand or respond?
- Who are your key stakeholders both internally and externally? Create a list.

- How can you describe each relationship? What do they look like? What do you need from the person? What does the person need from you?
- Think through this list based on the Emotional Bank Account concept (debits and credits).
- Add potential clients, decision-makers, influencers, and teachers (who will help you grow) to that list.
- Plan a breakfast/lunch and a lunch/dinner with two people and call/mail exchange with two people every week. Be consistent; it will compound. Be inspirational for and inspired by others.
- Create your gratitude journal. Write down 2 things and people you are grateful for every single day in your journal or on a Post-it and put it into a gratitude jar. The icing on the cake here is to review all your gratitude notes on 31 December and you will enter the New Year with elevated energy and a smile on your face and in your heart.

## TRUST – Self-Assessment

| |
|---|
| ☐ I trust my capabilities, my native genius, and my current and future potential as a leader. |
| ☐ I listen to my intuition when I make decisions. |
| ☐ I am open to being vulnerable by regularly sharing my mistakes and how I learnt from them. |
| ☐ I am a knowledgeable leader and always eager to expand my knowledge in the field of leadership. |
| ☐ I always keep my word and my promises. |

| |
|---|
| ☐ People can count on me. I am always there for them when they need me. They always have my support. |
| ☐ I value consistency over trendy. |
| ☐ I have a real human connection with the people in my team. |
| ☐ I actively listen to people without cynicism, judgement, or fear. |
| ☐ I have a daily routine to practise gratitude. |

If you marked 8 or more of the above statements as true for you, then you have probably mastered this quality.

Note the unmarked statements that you could still work on further enhancing this quality.

Write down the areas you want to work on based on the unmarked statements. brings you 80% results!

.......................................................................................................

.......................................................................................................

.......................................................................................................

.......................................................................................................

.......................................................................................................

Which statements did you find hard to respond to? Consider asking others for feedback.

.......................................................................................................

.......................................................................................................

.......................................................................................................

.......................................................................................................

## The pinnacle of your CRAFT journey

Answer these questions to become a CRAFTed REAL LEADER:

- What do you want to stand for as a leader?
- What is your way of being a CRAFTed leader?
- What is your unique edge?
- What makes you a powerful and unique leader?
- What kind of leader do you have the potential to become?
- What kind of leader do you want to become?

# CHAPTER VIII

# Outside Journey - Leading your organisation
# How do you steer your CRAFT?

"It is good to have an end to journey towards;
but it is the journey that matters, in the end."

(Ursula Le Guin, 1969)

## Putting into practice

Putting CRAFT Leadership into practice is a huge topic. If we wanted to explore it from every angle, it would take a long time to discuss all the related issues and challenges you may face, if as a leader you are committed to a long developmental journey. But given that we are coming to the end of this book, I suggest using a tool as a supporting mechanism here. This tool, besides mobilising the analytical and rational left hemisphere of your brain, also switches on the creative, and the more holistic right one. Not only does it widen the horizon, but it can also quickly grasp the essence of any topic and the nub of all the issues presented. What I am talking about here is the metaphor.

## The metaphor

The word *metaphor* comes from the Greek words *metaphora* and *metapherein* meaning transfer. Its modern meaning from the Oxford English Dictionary is "a figure of speech in which a name or descriptive word or phrase is transferred to an object or action different from, but analogous to, that to which it is literally applicable" and "a thing regarded as representative or symbolic of something else".

A metaphor can give deep and colourful insight into a leader's unique perception of their situation, their challenges, and their goals. Metaphors move beyond words, and open new uncovered, hidden areas and submerged dimensions. They are always full of colour and emotion. A metaphor simplifies situations and, at the same time invites many, sometimes previously unknown fresh perceptions into a conversation. It is like being on the ground (zoom in) and being on the helicopter (zoom out) at the same time. It is a unique and powerful discovery journey. The metaphor is quite common in everyday language; we sometimes use it unconsciously. Earlier in my career, I learnt how to intentionally notice and use metaphors as a professional. When I studied this topic back then, I was not even sure whether I could notice metaphors. Therefore, my first experiment was about watching out for metaphors, and noticing them in everyday conversations. The next step was when I mentioned to one of my clients that I would like to practise this area during our sessions. We had a lot of fun, as I accidentally picked a client who really was a 'metaphor person'. Because she also wanted to be helpful, she pointed out every time she used a metaphor. Since then, I have developed a great deal in this area and I am ever so grateful to my client for this learning experience.

Whether you are leading a team, making a presentation, or simply conversing with a colleague, metaphors play an important role and can be enormously inspirational and impactful in the workplace. Metaphors are also valuable tools in business, particularly when you need to explore and communicate complex and sometimes dry ideas. They are also necessary when you present your vision to capture both the mind and the heart of your people.

## Exploring your leadership with a metaphor

Let's use the metaphor of your being the captain of your CRAFT. Unfold your own story by using this metaphor with questions. Play with the CRAFT acronym by imagining a picture of you sailing a craft.

What kind of craft do you lead? What does it look like? How do you navigate your craft? How do you lead your organisation, your division, and your team? As a captain, how do you steer your craft? What direction are you sailing? How did you plan your sailing, your voyage? Do you have a plan B or C prepared? You have to train yourself to be resilient as well because when an unavoidable storm hits your craft you must adapt and adjust. The huge untamed water of the oceans makes every captain strong and humble at the same time. Are you practising the virtue of humility? How do you manoeuvre your craft out of and into harbours? What are the weather conditions? What kind of wind is blowing? A headwind or a tailwind? There are also specific winds you need to be aware of and prepared for like the Bora on the Adriatic Sea. You need to sharpen yourself for the wind, and steer your boat to take the wind out of the sails. How does the stormy weather influence the direction you are sailing in? When there is no wind, there is no moving. You should appreciate any winds as a captain. Ride them. Make the most of them. Create opportunities out of them. Are you fully present at the wheel on the deck or running on autopilot most of the time? What do you and your team do in calm, windless weather? How should you make the most of this period? Are you and your team resting, and when you do, how much energy do you waste while you are floating? Who is on board? How do you best allocate and delegate tasks to your crew?

When you are steering your craft on stormy waters you need to deliver very specific, clear communication. How do the teams work together on deck? How effectively and smoothly do you cooperate with various external stakeholders, for example when you are docking (marine workers, other crews)? You may also sail on international waters, or through the territories of several countries. You must abide not only by the rules of all of them, but you must also be diplomatic as is required in any multinational organisation.

What signals or lights do you need to use along the strait to make the journey safe for your organisation and others as well? What ethical behaviours are needed on the water you sail? How do you take care of your crew on board and make sure you don't jeopardise their wellbeing? How do you prevent them from burning out? When you chart your journey, how precisely do you know what to expect and how much will your leadership rely on your intuition and experience? Is there any competition on the ocean or the sea? How bloody is that competition? Can you find uncharted waters and undiscovered destinations? How sharp are you and your team to beat the competitors? Or rather, how can you make the competition irrelevant? How much do you and your leadership team enjoy sailing?

What can you rely on when you are sailing in the fog?

I could carry on exploring this metaphor along with or underneath the real story of leading an organisation. You've got the point though about how this metaphor can help you explore your own way of navigating and leading your craft into the future. Fair winds, Captain!

## Anecdote 6. What is floating on the clear blue water?

Let me share with you a little bit profane, maybe less presentable but a very powerful story of mine. I had an executive client who was a leader in a multinational organisation. The topic of our conversation was about vision, strategy, goals, what direction the organisation was heading, and what direction his team was heading. I felt that the conversation wasn't getting anywhere; we'd hit a wall. I detected quite a bit of suppressed frustration and anger in my client. He also shared with me that there was a kind of expectation from the regional leadership that they must 'sail so fast ahead on the clear blue water that they should leave their competitors behind'. When I started thinking about what kind of intervention I could use to make a shift, to break through this wall, the leader just blurted out: "You know Beáta, the problem with this whole thing is that there are huge pieces of shit floating around in the clear blue water." For a moment the air froze. 'Should I or should I not', I thought. I couldn't resist the temptation. "Tell me about those pieces of shit floating on the clear blue water! What do they look like? Where are you standing (sailing) in relation to those pieces of shit? What is beyond them? How do you envision the clear blue water?" We burst out laughing especially after I'd fired so many 'shitty' questions at him. When we started exploring it, we danced around the metaphor, which was pretty funny and quite intriguing. It was a picture of the very serious, tense reality of his leadership dilemmas. Because of the metaphor, our laughter liberated so much energy in my client that his creativity kicked in, and many layers of the conversation started unfolding. He learnt a lot about the water, the weather conditions, the sailing team, the colour of the oceans, and the disruptions in the surrounding waters. He learnt about himself as a leader, as a captain, about how he perceived and experienced that reality and how much of it he wished was ready to change.

If you are stuck with a leadership problem, or a topic, use the right hemisphere of your brain, use your creativity, and work with metaphors.

As a leader, what's your metaphor when you answer this question: What is it like leading your organisation/your team? You may come up with something totally different.

## The impact of your CRAFT Leadership

What is the impact of your CRAFT Leadership? Your journey is not only developing you, but through your learning, your team and your organisation advance as well. Never underestimate the impact of your actions and words (or lack of them). Remember, everything starts with you. Your choices and decisions influence not only your and your family's lives but the lives of all your employees, your stakeholders, and their families. Therefore, you cannot settle for good enough and mediocracy. You should strive for high-quality leadership. That is the only way to CRAFT your own future as a leader and CRAFT a sustainable future for all the people you are responsible for.

# CHAPTER IX

## Keep sharpening the REAL LEADER in you to be fit for the future

"Leadership and learning are indispensable to each other."
(John F. Kennedy, 1963)

### Reinforcing CRAFT Leadership

I am so proud of this baby of mine, CRAFT Leadership. Not only because I laboured through hundreds of conversations with leaders and executives, but also because it has lots of potential; it has been evolving beautifully. Like your leadership. That's not static either. Even if you have vast experience, it is still evolving, changing, and adapting to the current and future business environment. Leadership is a journey, not a destination.

**What makes you a unique and at the same time authentic leader? What makes you a powerful and confident leader?**

There is a reason why I pair uniqueness with authenticity. Uniqueness should never be artificial, fake, false, or untrue. Otherwise, you won't have any followers. In the same manner, you can't build your power only on external resources such as position, or masking, by pretending to be someone you are not. It should be built on a healthy and well-balanced confidence nurtured from the inside out.

This is all about a conscious decision on what kind of legacy you want to leave behind in the world. A clear picture with real, true meanings and key messages about yourself as a leader is your anchor in the stormy ocean of your life.

Successful leaders have a crystal-clear picture of their strengths and weaknesses. They know who they are and who they are not. And this is important! They don't try to become everything for everybody. They don't try to pretend. In their personality and in their behaviours – no matter whether they are at their workplace or at home – there is no discrepancy. They are honest. This lack of pretence is the reason why they can connect so well and easily with others.

So, I invite you to sharpen the REAL LEADER in you by mobilising your 5 CRAFT Leadership qualities to achieve breakthrough business results and success.

I started this journey by saying that today and tomorrow you must own qualities like CREATIVITY, RESILIENCE, AGILITY, FOCUS, and TRUST to meet the challenges of the unpredictable, continuously changing business environment. We've unfolded the details of these 5 qualities along with many questions that will help you find your own uniqueness and power as a leader. CRAFT is an acronym that is full of playfulness and creativity; it contains currently relevant and future-focused leadership messages and diverse development potential. It is no wonder I fell in love with it so passionately.

### *Keep sharpening the REAL LEADER in you*

But it doesn't stop here. Believe me, if you've worked through this book and come back to it again in a while, all those questions will open up more avenues, more potential than previously. You will see how this is an evolving journey and how you find new meaning, new insights by answering the same questions again and again.

Without continuously sharpening the REAL LEADER in you and working on these 5 leadership qualities you can easily lose your competitive edge as a leader. What do you need to do to keep yourself on your toes? People today want to follow leaders who are evolving more and more. They want to learn from leaders they see growing and learning. As nothing is permanent in business, nothing is permanent in leadership. You cannot afford not to keep sharpening and working particularly on the 5 CRAFT Leadership qualities.

- What is your CRAFT as a leader?
- What does it take to become a CRAFTed Leader?
- How can you build a CRAFTed Leadership Team?
- How can your key talents with leadership potential become CRAFTed Leaders?

My profession, no, my passion is to support you in finding answers to these questions.

There are two more things you can do as you embark on or continue on your development leadership journey:

1. **Daily reflection rituals (15 minutes)**: More productive and effective leaders have a high level of self-awareness, which cannot be achieved without regular daily reflection habits. When I worked for a multinational organisation I was rushing through my life. My calendar was always full. There was little or no space for self-reflection. Looking back now, I feel awfully sorry for missing out on so much learning and development, which could have been drawn from all the interactions, events, and actions I had. I could have seen things earlier before they hit me. I could have been more prepared for the challenges life presented to me. I always tell my executive clients: 'Have a notebook on your nightstand. Reflect on your day and jot down all the key learning points to remember before turning into bed. Because tomorrow will push yesterday's stuff away and you won't remember any of them.'

2. **Daily intentional development rituals (30 minutes):** The funny thing here is that many leaders expect their people to have a growth mindset and continuously develop themselves. But when I ask them how much time they spend on their learning and development, many of them say: 'Oh I am extremely busy, I am learning on the job a lot... etc.' You know what? Leadership is an evolving CRAFT in block capitals; it should be taught and studied diligently. But the tricky thing is, that it should be tailored to your specific needs because every leadership journey is uniquely different. I bet when you reply to the questions in this book and your peer replies to them too, your answers will be very different in words, in length, and in depth as well. My

experience shows that leaders from multinational organisations are gifted with many excellent training courses on leadership, and when I work with them, they have all the leadership and developmental terminologies in their heads. They can quote any of them easily and explain how it should look ideally. But when I dig deeper, what I have seen is that somehow, they find it hard to tailor all this knowledge to their specific needs, to internalise it and implement it in a way that makes them stronger and more REAL as a leader. Leaders from SMEs, on the other hand, have a vast amount of experience in leadership but very little knowledge due to the lack of formal training. Therefore, we need to spend a lot of time labelling their experience to be able to categorise their leadership experience as data so that we can raise their awareness and empower them by using those data again consciously when they lead. And these are only two of the specific patterns I recognised as different. There are many more not only at a group level but also at an individual level. So, make sure that you spend a minimum of 30 minutes per day reading books, completing exercises, and watching videos on leadership. Jot down your unique learning. Trust me, this 30-minute daily ritual will add up after a while, and the impact will compound.

## *What can the future hold for these 5 CRAFT Leadership qualities?*

What I see and what the leaders predicted during our interviews, is that our world, with its exponential growth and constant changes, requires leaders to be sharper than ever. They need to be more ahead of the game. They all agreed that the 5 CRAFT Leadership qualities are the fundamentals for their being able to do their job not only now but in the future, as well. They see more need for collaboration and partnership, which requires conscious and intentional TRUST-building. The unpredictability of today's world requires them to be closer to the market, to listen to the customers and respond to their needs not only faster, as it has limits, but more importantly smarter (AGILITY). This also requires relentless curiosity and openness to come up with creative and innovative solutions (CREATIVITY and CREATE). Inviting more shifting perspectives into business conversations and combining dichotomic forces requires all 5 CRAFT Leadership qualities to be in one place. According to one leader:

> "Our past routines will be overwritten by the present ad hoc, and the future will be built on this."

This begs the question of how to provide stability in this unstable and continuously changing environment. (This will take another book to explore in detail.) What to keep from the past, what legacy must be brought into the future, and how much should be constantly renewed? This can only be answered by laser-sharp FOCUS from leadership and with the much-needed deep wisdom coming from RESILIENCE in order not to lose your rock. As one leader noted:

> "The greatest challenge of the future is how to retain people by seeing their human uniqueness and not to view them as machines and economic figures."

This cannot be achieved without high-quality leadership. Because if you don't have people, you can throw your great strategy out of the window.

Are the leadership qualities explored in this book complete? No, definitely not. Will these leadership qualities be the same 5 years from now? No, definitely not. But these leadership qualities are essential not only to start but also to advance on the journey of becoming and being a high-quality leader. Evolution cannot be stopped, not even for 5 minutes. This book, therefore, is a snapshot of the 5 CRAFT Leadership qualities as of today.

## Anecdote 7. Personal closing story

When I was in high school, I studied English, but I was a complete failure. I hated the subject. My teachers made sure to remind me every time we had a lesson how much I didn't know. It blocked me, and as a result, I barely managed to get the lowest mark to pass my final exam. At that time, I didn't know that I was capable of learning English, writing in English, talking in English, running training courses in English, and even having insightful developmental coaching and mentoring conversations in English. I didn't even know how much I loved the English language. And here I am writing this book in English. No, not in Hungarian, in English. I am glad that I managed to unleash this potential of mine. Reading, studying leadership topics, and conversing with leaders from all over the world in English - that's made me who I am

Why am I telling you this? My answer is another story.

Some years ago, I had a client from a technology company. He felt stuck. He wasn't sure what his next move should be. He was uncertain whether the direction his company was heading at the time provided any appealing perspectives and challenges for him. We worked on several topics, but what was most interesting for me was that I saw far more potential in him than he saw in himself from the very beginning. Don't misunderstand me! He was a confident leader, but he had drawn a line for himself for some reason. We worked together for almost two and a half years. If I remember correctly, after a couple of sessions, when we talked about his plans, his vision for himself, I asked him why he didn't aim to become the managing director of this company? I thought he was great leadership material. He's eager to further improve himself. He not only had a strong grip and knowledge of leadership, and a hunger to make a company great and successful, but he also had humility and gratitude towards what he had achieved so far and towards the people and the company who had helped him to succeed. He said; he wasn't that type of leader'. He couldn't see himself doing it. I sensed a kind of disbelief in his capabilities and whether the events could unfold in a way to make it happen. In short, he couldn't see himself in that top position.

I asked the question once more during the first year of our work together and I let it go, although I believed in him and saw even more and more that he was absolutely capable. After one and a half years when we were just about closing the process, he asked me whether I could help him prepare for the role of being the managing director of 1,300 people. Much water has run in the Danube since then. He made major transformations, led the company through a spin-off merger, achieved great success, and became a regional managing director. And this was the leader who had not seen himself as a top leader of a huge multinational organisation. I am so proud of him!

We have much more in us than we can imagine. And your people have much more in them than they can imagine. I can only hope that this book is one of those that helps you unleash your hidden potential to make you a unique and authentic, strong and powerful leader by mobilising your 5 CRAFT Leadership qualities.

**Are you ready for your CRAFT Leadership journey, Captain?**

**Because this book was just the START....**

# REFERENCES

Accenture. (2019). Striking Balance with Whole Brain Leadership to achieve competitive agility. Retrieved from https://www.accenture.com/us-en/insights/strategy/whole-brain-leadership-for-c-suites [accessed 20 September 2021].

Aghdami, R. (2018). How to beat stress and burnout: Strategies for people under pressure. Workshop, Budapest, 17 October 2018. Coaching Határok Nélkül (CHN) [Coaching without Borders].

Angelou, M. (2014). You can't use up creativity, the more you see the more you have. New Classroom Motivational Poster. Retrieved from https://www.amazon.com/Maya-Angelou-Creativity-Classroom-Motivational/dp/B00IRDKRL4 [accessed 3 October 2021].

Blakey, J. (2016). *The Trusted Executive.* London: Kogan Page Limited. 225pp.

de Bono, E. (2017). *Six Thinking Hats*. London: Penguin Books. Kindle edition. 180pp.

Botsman, R. (2017). *Who Can You Trust?: How Technology Brought Us Together and Why It Might Drive Us Apart*. London: Penguin Random House Group. 336pp.

Bradberry, T. (2014), Multitasking damages your brain and career, new studies suggest. *Forbes*. Retrieved from https://www.forbes.com/sites/travisbradberry/2014/10/08/multitasking-damages-your-brain-and-career-new-studies-suggest/?sh=357d94fb56ee [accessed 20 September 2021].

Brown, A.C. & Waslien, C.I. (2003). Stress and Nutrition. In Caballero, B. (ed). *Encyclopedia of Food Sciences and Nutrition (Second Edition)* pp.5628–5636. Maryland: Academic Press. ISBN 978-0-12-227055-0.

Cambridge Dictionary. (n.d.). Definition of quality. Retrieved from https://dictionary.cambridge.org/dictionary/english/quality [accessed 2 November 2021].

Cambridge Dictionary. (n.d.). Definition of Creativity. Retrieved from https://dictionary.cambridge.org/dictionary/english/creativity [accessed 3 October 2021].

Center for Creative Leadership. (2020). How to boost brain health. Retrieved from https://www.ccl.org/articles/leading-effectively-articles/do-you-treat-your-brain-like-junk/ [accessed 1 November 2021].

Clark, K. B. & Wheelwright, S. C. (1993). *Managing New Product and Process Development: Text and Cases*. New York: Free Press. 896pp.

Covey, S. M. R. (2008). T*he Speed of Trust*. London: Simon & Schuster UK Ltd. 354pp.

Covey, R. S. (2004). *The 7 Habits of Highly Effective People*. New York: Simon & Schuster Inc. 178pp.

Crenshaw, D. (2021). *The Myth of Multitasking: How "Doing It All" Gets Nothing Done. 2nd Edition*. Miami, FL: Mango Publishing Group. 118pp.

Cuddy, A. (2012). Your body language may shape who you are. TEDGlobal 2012. Retrieved from https://www.ted.com/talks/amy_cuddy_your_body_language_may_shape_who_you_are [accessed 19 April 2022].

DDI. (2021). Global Leadership Forecast 2021. Retrieved from https://www.ddiworld.com/global-leadership-forecast-2021 [accessed 19 April 2022].

Edelman. (2021). 2021 Edelman Trust Barometer. https://www.edelman.com/trust/2021-trust-barometer [accessed 5 October 2021].

Eggers, J. & Barlow, C. (2019). *Resilience: It's Not About Bouncing Back: How Leaders and Organizations Can Build Resilience Before Disruption Hits*. Pasadena, CA: Best Seller Publishing, LLC. 255pp.

Erikson, T. (2019). *Surrounded by Idiots: The Four Types of Human Behavior and How to Effectively Communicate with Each in Business (and in Life)*. New York: St. Martin's Essentials. 293pp.

Fodor, L. (2007). A kreatív személyiség [The creative personality]. *Közoktatás* 18 (7):4–6.

Gapingvoid. (2019). How to be a successful CEO. Retrieved from https://www.gapingvoid.com/blog/2019/03/14/how-to-be-a-successful-ceo/ [accessed 20 September 2021].

de Geus, A. (1988). Planning as Learning. *Harvard Business Review*. Retrieved from https://hbr.org/1988/03/planning-as-learning [accessed 23 October 2021].

Gorlick, A. & Hubbard, J. (2009). Multitasking works? Not really, Stanford study shows. Retrieved from. https://news.stanford.edu/news/2009/august24/videos/605.html [accessed 11 February 2022].

Guilford, J. P. (1950). Creativity. *American Psychologist* 5:444–454.

Hall, D. J. (2017). Think again: The Strategic Role of Creativity. Workshop, Budapest, 29 November 2017. Coaching Határok Nélkül (CHN) [Coaching without Borders].

Hanse, E. C. & Carucci, R. A. (2014). *Rising to Power: The Journey of Exceptional Executives.* Austin, TX: Greenleaf Book Group Press. 296pp.

Hayward, S. (2018). *The Agile Leader: How to Create an Agile Business in the Digital Age.* London: Kogan Page. 224pp.

Ideas Centre Group. (nd.). Lego and Superheroes creativity techniques. Retrieved from https://www.ideascentregroup.com/resources/free-videos/techniques/ [accessed 25 February 2022].

Full Potential Group. (2020). Improve agility, performance and well-being. Retrieved from https://fullpotentialgroup.com/product/improve-agility-performance-and-well-being/ [accessed 2 November 2021].

Jawad, A. Q. & Kakabadse, A. (2019). *Leadership Intelligence.* New York: Bloomsbury Publishing Plc. p113.

Johnson, W. (2015). *Disrupt Yourself: Putting the Power of Disruptive Innovation to Work.* New York: Bibliomotion, Inc. 208pp.

Kennedy, J. F. (1963). Remarks prepared for delivery at the Trade Mart in Dallas, Tx. Retrieved from https://www.jfklibrary.org/archives/other-resources/john-f-kennedy-speeches/dallas-tx-trade-mart-undelivered-19631122 [accessed 30 March 2022].

Kim, W. C. & Mauborgne, R. (2005). *Blue Ocean Strategy: How to Create Uncontested Market Space and Make Competition Irrelevant.* Boston, MA: Harvard Business School Publishing Corporation. 256pp.

Kim, W. C. & Mauborgne. R. (2017). *Blue Ocean Shift: Beyond Competing – Proven Steps to Inspire Confidence and Seize New Growth*. New York: Hachette Book Group, Inc. 336pp.

Koch. R. (2011): *The 80/20 Principle: The Secret to Achieving More with Less.* New York: Currency. 336pp.

Kouchaki, M. & Smith, I. H. (2013): The Morning Morality Effect: The influence of time of day on unethical behaviour. *Psychological Science*, 25(1):95–102. Retrieved from http://journals.sagepub.com/doi/abs/10.1177/0956797613498099 [accessed 30 March 2022].

Le Guin, U. K. (1969). *The Left Hand of Darkness.* New York: Ace Books. Ch15.

Lencioni, P. M. (2005). *Overcoming the Five Dysfunctions of a Team: A Field Guide for Leaders, Managers, and Facilitators* (J-B Lencioni Series Book 44). San Francisco, CA: Jossey-Bass. 154pp.

Lexico. (n.d.) Definition of Agility. Retrieved from https://www.lexico.com/definition/agility [accessed 23 October 2021].

Loehr, J. & Schwartz, T. (2003). *The Power of Full Engagement: Managing Energy, not Time, is the Key to High Performance and Personal Renewal.* New York: Free Press. 245pp.

Maister, D., Galford, R., & Green, C. (2002). *The Trusted Advisor.* London. Simon & Schuster UK Ltd. 240pp.

Maxwell, J. C. (2018). *Developing the Leader Within You 2.0.* Nashville, TN: HarperCollins Leadership. p16.

Maxwell, J. C. (2015): *The Leadership Handbook: 26 Critical Lessons Every Leader Needs.* Nashville, TN: Nelson Books. p98.

Maxwell, J. C. (2013): *The 5 Levels of Leadership.* New York: Center Street. 304pp.

Maxwell, J. C. (2007). *The 21 Irrefutable Laws of Leadership.* Nashville, TN: HarperCollins Leadership. p11.

McDowell-Larsen, S. (2016). The care and feeding of the leader's brain. White Paper. Center of Creative Leadership. Retrieved from https://www.ccl.org/wp-content/uploads/2015/04/CareFeedingLeadersBrain.pdf [accessed 2 November 2021].

Mejia, Z. (2018). Steve Jobs: Here's what most people get wrong about focus. *CNBC,* 2 October. Retrieved from https://www.cnbc.com/2018/10/02/steve-jobs-heres-what-most-people-get-wrong-about-focus.html [accessed 30 March 2022].

Morgan, J. (2020). *The Future Leader.* Hoboken, NJ: John Wiley & Sons, Inc., 320pp.

Nixon, N. (2020). *The Creativity Leap: Unleash Curiosity, Improvisation, and Intuition at Work.* Oakland, CA: Berrett-Koehler Publisher, Inc. 224pp.

Oxford Dictionary. (n.d.). Definition of metaphor. Retrieved from https://www.oed.com/view/Entry/117328?redirectedFrom=metaphor [accessed 25 November 2021].

PwC. (2021). CEO Survey 2021 Hungary & Global Data on Figure of 'Which of the following activities, if any, are you planning in the next 12 months in order to drive corporate growth or profitability?' Retrieved from https://www.pwc.com/hu/en/kiadvanyok/assets/pdf/PwC-CEO_Survey_2021-EN.pdf [accessed 23 October 2021].

Scharmer, C.O. (2018). *The Essentials of Theory U: Core Principles and Applications.* Oakland, CA: Berrett-Koehler Publishers. 192pp.

Schwab, K. (2015). Are you ready for the technology revolution? World Economic Forum. Retrieved from https://www.weforum.org/agenda/2015/02/are-you-ready-for-the-technological-revolution/ [accessed 30 March 2022].

Scotton, N. & Scott, A. (2017). *The Little Book of Making Big Change Happen.* Market Harborough, Leics: Matador. 122pp.

Selye, H. (1951). The General-Adaptation-Syndrome. *Annual Review of Medicine,* 2:327–342. Retrieved from https://doi.org/10.1146/annurev.me.02.020151.001551 [accessed 30 March 2022].

Simpson, G.K. & Yuen, F.K. (2018). *Contemporary Perspectives on Social Work in Acquired Brain Injury.* London: Routledge. 254pp.

Sinek, S. (2014). *Leaders Eat Last: Why Some Teams Pull Together and Others Don't.* New York: Penguin Group (USA) Inc. 368pp.

Trusted Advisor (n.d.). The Trusted Advisor Equation: Trusted Advisor Associates LLC. Retrieved from https://trustedadvisor.com/articles/the-trust-equation-a-primer [accessed 1 December 2021].

Venkatraman, R. (2018). You're 96 percent less creative than you were as a child. Here's how to reverse that. *Inc.* Retrieved from https://www.inc.com/rohini-venkatraman/4-ways-to-get-back-creativity-you-had-as-a-kid.html [accessed 7 April 2022].

Vermeulen, A. (2018). Neuro-Agility Profile™ Practitioner Training and Course material by Neuro-Link Global. Self-paced learning programme. Available at https://neurolink.company/cms/brain-profile-practitioner-training-program/ [accessed 19 April 2022].

Visual Paradigm Online. (n.d.). Pareto analysis using Pareto Principle 28/80 rules. Retrieved from https://online.visual-paradigm.com/knowledge/pareto-chart/pareto-analysis-using-pareto-principle-20-80-rules/ [accessed 30 September 2021].

Whiting, K. (2020). These are the top 10 job skills of tomorrow – and how long it takes to learn them. WeForum. Retrieved from https://www.weforum.org/agenda/2020/10/top-10-work-skills-of-tomorrow-how-long-it-takes-to-learn-them/ [accessed 22 October 2021].

Williamson, J. N. (1986). *The Leader-Manager.* New York: John Wiley and Sons. p149.

Wiseman, L. (2017). *Multipliers, Revised and Updated: How the Best Leaders Make Everyone Smarter.* New York: Harper Business. 457pp.

Witzel, M. (2019). *The Ethical Leader: Why Doing the Right Thing Can Be the Key to Competitive Advantage.* London: Bloomsbury Business. p184.

# LIST OF ILLUSTRATIONS

## List of Figures


Figure 1.1: The 4 DISC behavioural styles 15
Figure 1.2: Key descriptors of high-intensity DISC behavioural styles 17
Figure 1.3: Authenticity in the overlap 26
Figure 1.4: CRAFT Leadership 40
Figure 2.1: The CREATIVITY Cocktail 52
Figure 2.2: The ERRC grid 70
Figure 3.1: General Adaptation Syndrome 83
Figure 4.1: Measuring the quantity of physical energy on a scale of 1 to 10 110
Figure 4.2: Measuring the quality of emotional energy on a scale of 1 to 10 111
Figure 4.3: Measuring the focus of mental energy on a scale of 1 to 10 112
Figure 4.4: Measuring shifts in spiritual energy on a scale of 1 to 10 113
Figure 4.5: The sequence of effective energy management 113
Figure 5.1: Example dashboard of the 7 Factors that Impact Our Neurological Design 134
Figure 5.2: Example of a brain-optimising dashboard, which contains the 6 drivers to optimise your brain performance 138
Figure 6.1: Functionality dimensions of leadership FOCUS 154
Figure 6.2: Task allocation in the functionality dimension of Leadership FOCUS 155
Figure 6.3: The Pareto Principle - 80% of the outputs result from 20% of the inputs 160
Figure 6.4: Four major types of systemic patterns 166
Figure 7.1: The Trust Equation 197
Figure 8.1: CRAFT Leadership 224

## List of Tables

Table 2.1: Ingredient #1 - Ignite and cultivate curiosity within yourself and in your teams 53
Table 2.2: Ingredient #2 – Endure discomfort 58
Table 2.3: Ingredient #3 – Be persistent and disciplined 63

## List of Mind Maps

CREATIVITY and CREATE Mind Map 226
RESILIENCE Mind Map 230
AGILITY Mind Map 234
FOCUS Mind Map 238
TRUST Mind Map 244

# ABOUT THE AUTHOR

As a Transformational and Leadership Expert, Executive Coach, and Speaker, Beáta Kalamár provides invaluable personalised support to leaders tackling a wide scale of complex challenges and uncertainties in today's global business market. She takes pride in her clients accomplishing their business and career goals and supports them to become the authors of their own success stories. Her mission is not only to create her signature presence but also to support leaders in creating their own leadership signature presence and legacy by making a difference and stimulating long-lasting change and transformation in themselves and others.

Internationally accredited by the International Coaching Federation, Beáta also holds a degree in Andragogy. She obtained her Practitioner Diploma in Executive Coaching from the Academy of Executive Coaching (UK) and is certified by Success Insights CEE as a Professional Value and Behavioural Analyst and Consultant (CPVA and CPBA). Beáta also works as a 360 Degree and BEI (Behavioural Event Interview) Feedback Consultant. She supports executives to remain competitive in the market as an Accredited Licensed Practitioner of Neuro-Agility Profile™ (NAP™) by increasing their level of adaptability and change agility to be able to constantly renew themselves.

With more than 20 years of experience in individual and team coaching in multinational organisations, her clients include business owners, entrepreneurs, C-Suite executives, leadership team members, directors, high-potential senior managers, and managers. She has worked with some of the most prestigious organisations in a variety of businesses in Hungary and Central and Eastern Europe (CEE) including 10 years with PwC Hungary and CEE as an internal executive coach, trainer, and L&D manager.

She was elected to be the President of the Hungarian Chapter of the International Coaching Federation for 2014 – a non-profit organisation of 120 members. Beáta not only believes in lifelong learning and continuous renewal of self, she practises daily as well.

For further information about her work, visit her website www.beatakalamar.com. To obtain a Neuro-Agility™ Profile - Advanced+ Report and find out how you can activate Neuro-Agility, contact Beáta at craftleadership@beatakalamar.com. Your Neuro-Agility Profile will provide you with invaluable insights to measure and track your performance, flexibility, and agility.